The Poetry of Emma Lazarus
Volume 3

Emma Lazarus was born on July 22nd, 1849, in New York City, the fourth of seven children of Moses Lazarus and Esther Nathan, Sephardic Jews whose families, originally from Portugal, had settled in New York during the colonial period.

From an early age, she studied American and British literature, as well as the German, French, and Italian languages. Her early writings attracted the attention of Ralph Waldo Emerson.

Emma grew to become not only an important poet but also edited many collections of German poems, including Johann Wolfgang von Goethe and Heinrich Heine, some of which we include in these volumes.

Among her other writings are a novel and two plays in five acts, 'The Spagnoletto', a tragic verse drama and 'The Dance to Death', a dramatization of a German short story about the burning of Jews in Nordhausen during the Black Death.

Her interest in her Jewish ancestry grew markedly after reading George Eliot's 'Daniel Deronda', together with the alarming reports of the Russian pogroms following the assassination of Tsar Alexander II in 1881. As a result of this appalling anti-Semitic violence, thousands of destitute Ashkenazi Jews left Russia for New York, leading Lazarus to write articles on the subject as well as the book 'Songs of a Semite' (1882).

She began to help on a more practical level by helping to establish the Hebrew Technical Institute in New York, to provide support, resources and vocational training to help destitute Jewish immigrants become self-supporting.

Emma's best known work is "The New Colossus", a sonnet written in 1883; its lines appear on a bronze plaque in the pedestal of the Statue of Liberty placed there in 1903. It was written for and donated to an auction, conducted by the "Art Loan Fund Exhibition in Aid of the Bartholdi Pedestal Fund for the Statue of Liberty" to raise funds to build the pedestal.

In the latter part of her second trip to Europe (1885 to 1887), she fell seriously ill, it is thought with Hodgkin's lymphoma, and returned to New York City. Emma Lazarus died two months later on November 19, 1887. She is buried in Beth-Olom Cemetery in Brooklyn.

She was an important forerunner of the Zionist movement and argued for the creation of a Jewish homeland thirteen years before Theodor Herzl began to use the term Zionism.

Emma was honored by the Office of the Manhattan Borough President in March 2008 and her home on West 10th Street is included in a map of Women's Rights Historic Sites.

Index Of Poems

Tannhauser

The Landgrave Hermann held a gathering
Of minstrels, minnesingers, troubadours,
At Wartburg in his palace, and the knight,
Sir Tannhauser of France, the greatest bard,
Inspired with heavenly visions, and endowed
With apprehension and rare utterance
Of noble music, fared in thoughtful wise
Across the Horsel meadows. Full of light,
And large repose, the peaceful valley lay,
In the late splendor of the afternoon,
And level sunbeams lit the serious face
Of the young knight, who journeyed to the west,
Towards the precipitous and rugged cliffs,
Scarred, grim, and torn with savage rifts and chasms,
That in the distance loomed as soft and fair
And purple as their shadows on the grass.
The tinkling chimes ran out athwart the air,
Proclaiming sunset, ushering evening in,
Although the sky yet glowed with yellow light.
The ploughboy, ere he led his cattle home,
In the near meadow, reverently knelt,
And doffed his cap, and duly crossed his breast,
Whispering his 'Ave Mary,' as he heard
The pealing vesper-bell. But still the knight,
Unmindful of the sacred hour announced,
Disdainful or unconscious, held his course.
'Would that I also, like yon stupid wight,
Could kneel and hail the Virgin and believe!'
He murmured bitterly beneath his breath.
'Were I a pagan, riding to contend
For the Olympic wreath, O with what zeal,
What fire of inspiration, would I sing
The praises of the gods! How may my lyre
Glorify these whose very life I doubt?
The world is governed by one cruel God,
Who brings a sword, not peace. A pallid Christ,

Unnatural, perfect, and a virgin cold,
They give us for a heaven of living gods,
Beautiful, loving, whose mere names were song;
A creed of suffering and despair, walled in
On every side by brazen boundaries,
That limit the soul's vision and her hope
To a red hell or and unpeopled heaven.
Yea, I am lost already, even now
Am doomed to flaming torture for my thoughts.
O gods! O gods! where shall my soul find peace?'
He raised his wan face to the faded skies,
Now shadowing into twilight; no response
Came from their sunless heights; no miracle,
As in the ancient days of answering gods.
With a long, shuddering sigh he glanced to earth,
Finding himself among the Horsel cliffs.
Gray, sullen, gaunt, they towered on either side;
Scant shrubs sucked meagre life between the rifts
Of their huge crags, and made small darker spots
Upon their wrinkled sides; the jaded horse
Stumbled upon loose, rattling, fallen stones,
Amidst the gathering dusk, and blindly fared
Through the weird, perilous pass. As darkness waxed,
And an oppressive mystery enwrapped
The roadstead and the rocks, Sir Tannhauser
Fancied he saw upon the mountain-side
The fluttering of white raiment. With a sense
Of wild joy and horror, he gave pause,
For his sagacious horse that reeked of sweat,
Trembling in every limb, confirmed his thought,
That nothing human scaled that haunted cliff.
The white thing seemed descending, now a cloud
It looked, and now a rag of drifted mist,
Torn in the jagged gorge precipitous,
And now an apparition clad in white,
Shapely and real, then he lost it quite,
Gazing on nothing with blank, foolish face.
As with wide eyes he stood, he was aware
Of a strange splendor at his very side,
A presence and a majesty so great,
That ere he saw, he felt it was divine.
He turned, and, leaping from his horse, fell prone,
In speechless adoration, on the earth,
Before the matchless goddess, who appeared
With no less freshness of immortal youth
Than when first risen from foam of Paphian seas.
He heard delicious strains of melody,
Such as his highest muse had ne'er attained,
Float in the air, while in the distance rang,
Harsh and discordant, jarring with those tones,
The gallop of his frightened horse's hoofs,

Clattering in sudden freedom down the pass.
A voice that made all music dissonance
Then thrilled through heart and flesh of that prone knight,
Triumphantly: 'The gods need but appear,
And their usurped thrones are theirs again!'
Then tenderly: 'Sweet knight, I pray thee, rise;
Worship me not, for I desire thy love.
Look on me, follow me, for I am fain
Of thy fair, human face.' He rose and looked,
Stirred by that heavenly flattery to the soul.
Her hair, unbraided and unfilleted,
Rained in a glittering shower to the ground,
And cast forth lustre. Round her zone was clasped
The scintillant cestus, stiff with flaming gold,
Thicker with restless gems than heaven with stars.
She might have flung the enchanted wonder forth;
Her eyes, her slightest gesture would suffice
To bind all men in blissful slavery.
She sprang upon the mountain's dangerous side,
With feet that left their print in flowers divine,
Flushed amaryllis and blue hyacinth,
Impurpled amaranth and asphodel,
Dewy with nectar, and exhaling scents
Richer than all the roses of mid-June.
The knight sped after her, with wild eyes fixed
Upon her brightness, as she lightly leapt
From crag to crag, with flying auburn hair,
Like a gold cloud, that lured him ever on,
Higher and higher up the haunted cliff.
At last amidst a grove of pines she paused,
Until he reached her, breathing hard with haste,
Delight, and wonder. Then upon his hand
She placed her own, and all his blood at once
Tingled and hotly rushed to brow and cheek,
At the supreme caress; but the mere touch
Infused fresh life, and when she looked at him
With gracious tenderness, he felt himself
Strong suddenly to bear the blinding light
Of those great eyes. 'Dear knight,' she murmured low,
'For love of me, wilt thou accord this boon,
To grace my weary home in banishment?'
His hungry eyes gave answer ere he spoke,
In tones abrupt that startled his own ears
With their strange harshness; but with thanks profuse
She guided him, still holding his cold hand
In her warm, dainty palm, unto a cave,
Whence a rare glory issued, and a smell
Of spice and roses, frankincense and balm.
They entering stood within a marble hall,
With straight, slim pillars, at whose farther end
The goddess led him to a spiral flight

Of stairs, descending always 'midst black gloom
Into the very bowels of the earth.
Down these, with fearful swiftness, they made way,
The knight's feet touching not the solid stair,
But sliding down as in a vexing dream,
Blind, feeling but that hand divine that still
Empowered him to walk on empty air.
Then he was dazzled by a sudden blaze,
In vast palace filled with reveling folk.
Cunningly pictured on the ivory walls
Were rolling hills, cool lakes, and boscage green,
And all the summer landscape's various pomp.
The precious canopy aloft was carved
In semblance of the pleached forest trees,
Enameled with the liveliest green, wherethrough
A light pierced, more resplendent than the day.
O'er the pale, polished jasper of the floor
Of burnished metal, fretted and embossed
With all the marvelous story of her birth
Painted in prodigal splendor of rich tincts,
And carved by heavenly artists, crystal seas,
And long-haired Nereids in their pearly shells,
And all the wonder of her lucent limbs
Sphered in a vermeil mist. Upon the throne
She took her seat, the knight beside her still,
Singing on couches of fresh asphodel,
And the dance ceased, and the flushed revelers came
In glittering phalanx to adore their queen.
Beautiful girls, with shining delicate heads,
Crested with living jewels, fanned the air
With flickering wings from naked shoulders soft.
Then with preluding low, a thousand harps,
And citherns, and strange nameless instruments,
Sent through the fragrant air sweet symphonies,
And the winged dancers waved in mazy rounds,
With changing lustres like a summer sea.
Fair boys, with charming yellow hair crisp-curled,
And frail, effeminate beauty, the knight saw,
But of strong, stalwart men like him were none.
He gazed thereon bewitched, until the hand
Of Venus, erst withdrawn, now fell again
Upon his own, and roused him from his trance.
He looked on her, and as he looked, a cloud
Auroral, flaming as at sunrising,
Arose from nothing, floating over them
In luminous folds, like that vermilion mist
Penciled upon the throne, and as it waxed
In density and brightness, all the throng
Of festal dancers, less and less distinct,
Grew like pale spirits in a vague, dim dream,
And vanished altogether; and these twain,

Shut from the world in that ambrosial cloud,
Now with a glory inconceivable,
Vivid and conflagrant, looked each on each.

All hours came laden with their own delights
In that enchanted place, wherein Time
Knew no divisions harsh of night and day,
But light was always, and desire of sleep
Was satisfied at once with slumber soft,
Desire of food with magical repast,
By unseen hands on golden tables spread.
But these the knight accepted like a god,
All less was lost in that excess of joy,
The crowning marvel of her love for him,
Assuring him of his divinity.
Meanwhile remembrance of the earth appeared
Like the vague trouble of a transient dream,
The doubt, the scruples, the remorse for thoughts
Beyond his own control, the constant thirst
For something fairer than his life, more real
Than airy revelations of his Muse.
Here was his soul's desire satisfied.
All nobler passions died; his lyre he flung
Recklessly forth, with vows to dedicate
His being to herself. She knew and seized
The moment of her mastery, and conveyed
The lyre beyond his sight and memory.
With blandishment divine she changed for him,
Each hour, her mood; a very woman now,
Fantastic, voluble, affectionate,
And jealous of the vague, unbodied air,
Exacting, penitent, and pacified,
All in a breath. And often she appeared
Majestic with celestial wrath, with eyes
That shot forth fire, and a heavy brow,
Portentous as the lowering front of heaven,
When the reverberant, sullen thunder rolls
Among the echoing clouds. Thus she denounced
Her ancient, fickle worshippers, who left
Her altars desecrate, her fires unfed,
Her name forgotten. 'But I reign, I reign!'
She would shrill forth, triumphant; 'yea, I reign.
Men name me not, but worship me unnamed,
Beauty and Love within their heart of hearts;
Not with bent knees and empty breath of words,
But with devoted sacrifice of lives.'
Then melting in a moment, she would weep
Ambrosial tears, pathetic, full of guile,
Accusing her own base ingratitude,
In craving worship, when she had his heart,
Her priceless knight, her peerless paladin,

Her Tannhauser; then, with an artful glance
Of lovely helplessness, entreated him
Not to desert her, like the faithless world,
For these unbeautiful and barbarous gods,
Or she would never cease her prayers to Jove,
Until he took from her the heavy curse
Of immortality. With closer vows,
The knight then sealed his worship and forswore
All other aims and deeds to serve her cause.
Thus passed unnoted seven barren years
Of reckless passion and voluptuous sloth,
Undignified by any lofty thought
In his degraded mind, that sometime was
Endowed with noble capability.
From revelry to revelry he passed,
Craving more pungent pleasure momently,
And new intoxications, and each hour
The siren goddess answered his desires.
Once when she left him with a weary sense
Of utter lassitude, he sat alone,
And, raising listless eyes, he saw himself
In a great burnished mirror, wrought about
With cunning imagery of twisted vines.
He scarcely knew those sunken, red-rimmed eyes,
For his who in the flush of manhood rode
Among the cliffs, and followed up the crags
The flying temptress; and there fell on him
A horror of her beauty, a disgust
For his degenerate and corrupted life,
With irresistible, intense desire,
To feel the breath of heaven on his face.
Then as Fate willed, who rules above the gods,
He saw, within the glass, behind him glide
The form of Venus. Certain of her power,
She had laid by, in fond security,
The enchanted cestus, and Sir Tannhauser,
With surfeited regard, beheld her now,
No fairer than the women of the earth,
Whom with serenity and health he left,
Duped by a lovely witch. Before he moved,
She knew her destiny; and when he turned,
He seemed to drop a mask, disclosing thus
An alien face, and eyes with vision true,
That for long time with glamour had been blind.
Hiding the hideous rage within her breast,
With girlish simpleness of folded hands,
Auroral blushes, and sweet, shamefast mien,
She spoke: 'Behold, my love, I have cast forth
All magic, blandishments and sorcery,
For I have dreamed a dream so terrible,
That I awoke to find my pillow stained

With tears as of real woe. I thought my belt,
By Vulcan wrought with matchless skill and power,
Was the sole bond between us; this being doffed,
I seemed to thee an old, unlovely crone,
Wrinkled by every year that I have seen.
Thou turnedst from me with a brutal sneer,
So that I woke with weeping. Then I rose,
And drew the glittering girdle from my zone,
Jealous thereof, yet full of fears, and said,
'If it be this he loves, then let him go!
I have no solace as a mortal hath,
No hope of change or death to comfort me
Through all eternity; yet he is free,
Though I could hold him fast with heavy chains,
Bound in perpetual imprisonment.'
Tell me my vision was a baseless dream;
See, I am kneeling, and kiss thy hands,
In pity, look on me, before thy word
Condemns me to immortal misery!'
As she looked down, the infernal influence
Worked on his soul again; for she was fair
Beyond imagination, and her brow
Seemed luminous with high self-sacrifice.
He bent and kissed her head, warm, shining, soft,
With its close-curling gold, and love revived.

But ere he spoke, he heard the distant sound
Of one sweet, smitten lyre, and a gleam
Of violent anger flashed across the face
Upraised to his in feigned simplicity
And singleness of purpose. Then he sprang,
Well-nigh a god himself, with sudden strength
To vanquish and resist, beyond her reach,
Crying, 'My old Muse calls me, and I hear!
Thy fateful vision is no baseless dream;
I will be gone from this accursed hall!'
Then she, too, rose, dilating over him,
And sullen clouds veiled all her rosy limbs,
Unto her girdle, and her head appeared
Refulgent, and her voice rang wrathfully:
'Have I cajoled and flattered thee till now,
To lose thee thus! How wilt thou make escape?
ONCE BEING MINE THOU ART FOREVER MINE:
Yea, not my love, but my poor slave and fool.'
But he, with both hands pressed upon his eyes,
Against that blinding lustre, heeded not
Her thundered words, and cried in sharp despair,
'Help me, O Virgin Mary! and thereat,
The very bases of the hall gave way,
The roof was rived, the goddess disappeared,
And Tannhauser stood free upon the cliff,

Amidst the morning sunshine and fresh air.

Around him were the tumbled blocks and crags,
Huge ridges and sharp juts of flinty peaks,
Black caves, and masses of the grim, bald rock.
The ethereal, unfathomable sky,
Hung over him, the valley lay beneath,
Dotted with yellow hayricks, that exhaled
Sweet, healthy odors to the mountain-top.
He breathed intoxicate the infinite air,
And plucked the heather blossoms where they blew,
Reckless with light and dew, in crannies green,
And scarcely saw their darling bells for tears.
No sounds of labor reached him from the farms
And hamlets trim, nor from the furrowed glebe;
But a serene and sabbath stillness reigned,
Till broken by the faint, melodious chimes
Of the small village church that called to prayer.
He hurried down the rugged, scarped cliff,
And swung himself from shelving granite slopes
To narrow foot-holds, near wide-throated chasms,
Tearing against the sharp stones his bleeding hands,
With long hair flying from his dripping brow,
Uncovered head, and white, exalted face.
No memory had he of his smooth ascent,
No thought of fear upon those dreadful hills;
He only heard the bell, inviting him
To satisfy the craving of his heart,
For worship 'midst his fellow men. He reached
The beaten, dusty road, and passed thereon
The pious peasants faring towards the church,
And scarce refrained from greeting them like friends
Dearly beloved, after long absence met.
How more than fair the sunburnt wenches looked,
In their rough, homespun gowns and coifs demure,
After the beauty of bare, rosy limbs,
And odorous, loose hair! He noted not
Suspicious glances on his garb uncouth,
His air extravagant and face distraught,
With bursts of laughter from the red-cheeked boys,
And prudent crossings of the women's breasts.
He passed the flowering close about the church,
And trod the well worn-path, with throbbing heart,
The little heather-bell between his lips,
And his eyes fastened on the good green grass.
Thus entered he the sanctuary, lit
With frequent tapers, and with sunbeams stained
Through painted glass. How pure and innocent
The waiting congregation seemed to him,
Kneeling, or seated with calm brows upraised!
With faltering strength, he cowered down alone,

And held sincere communion with the Lord,
For one brief moment, in a sudden gush
Of blessed tears. The minister of God
Rose to invoke a blessing on his flock,
And then began the service, not in words
To raise the lowly, and to heal the sick,
But an alien tongue, with phrases formed,
And meaningless observances. The knight,
Unmoved, yet thirsting for the simple word
That might have moved him, held his bitter thoughts,
But when in his own speech a new priest spake,
Looked up with hope revived, and heard the text:
'Go, preach the Gospel unto all the world.
He that believes and is baptized, is saved.
He that believeth not, is damned in hell!'
He sat with neck thrust forth and staring eyes;
The crowded congregation disappeared;
He felt alone in some black sea of hell,
While a great light smote one exalted face,
Vivid already with prophetic fire,
Whose fatal mouth now thundered forth his doom.
He longed in that void circle to cry out,
With one clear shriek, but sense and voice seemed bound,
And his parched tongue clave useless to his mouth.
As the last words resounded through the church,
And once again the pastor blessed his flock,
Who, serious and subdued, passed slowly down
The arrow aisle, none noted, near the wall,
A fallen man with face upon his knees,
A heap of huddled garments and loose hair,
Unconscious 'mid the rustling, murmurous stir,
'Midst light and rural smell of grass and flowers,
Let in athwart the doorway. One lone priest,
Darkening the altar lights, moved noiselessly,
Now with the yellow glow upon his face,
Now a black shadow gliding farther on,
Amidst the smooth, slim pillars of hewn ash.
But from the vacant aisles he heard at once
A hollow sigh, heaved from a depth profound.
Upholding his last light above his head,
And peering eagerly amidst the stalls,
He cried, 'Be blest who cometh in God's name.'
Then the gaunt form of Tannhauser arose.
'Father, I am a sinner, and I seek
Forgiveness and help, by whatso means
I can regain the joy of peace with God.'
'The Lord hath mercy on the penitent.
'Although thy sins be scarlet,' He hath said,
'Will I not make them white as wool?' Confess,
And I will shrive you.' Thus the good priest moved
Towards the remorseful knight and pressed his hand.

But shrinking down, he drew his fingers back
From the kind palm, and kissed the friar's feet.
'Thy pure hand is anointed, and can heal.
The cool, calm pressure brings back sanity,
And what serene, past joys! yet touch me not,
My contact is pollution, hear, O hear,
While I disburden my charged soul.' He lay,
Casting about for words and strength to speak.
'O father, is there help for such a one,'
In tones of deep abasement he began,
'Who hath rebelled against the laws of God,
With pride no less presumptuous than his
Who lost thereby his rank in heaven?' 'My son,
There is atonement for all sins, or slight
Or difficult, proportioned to the crime.
Though this may be the staining of thy hands
With blood of kinsmen or of fellow-men.'
'My hands are white, my crime hath found no name,
This side of hell; yet though my heart-strings snap
To live it over, let me make the attempt.
I was a knight and bard, with such a gift
Of revelation that no hour of life
Lacked beauty and adornment, in myself
The seat and centre of all happiness.
What inspiration could my lofty Muse
Draw from those common and familiar themes,
Painted upon the windows and the walls
Of every church, the mother and her child,
The miracle and mystery of the birth,
The death, the resurrection? Fool and blind!
That saw not symbols of eternal truth
In that grand tragedy and victory,
Significant and infinite as life.
What tortures did my skeptic soul endure,
At war against herself and all mankind!
The restless nights of feverish sleeplessness,
With balancing of reasons nicely weighed;
The dawn that brought no hope nor energy,
The blasphemous arraignment of the Lord,
Taxing His glorious divinity
With all the grief and folly of the world.
Then came relapses into abject fear,
And hollow prayer and praise from craven heart.
Before a sculptured Venus I would kneel,
Crown her with flowers, worship her, and cry,
'O large and noble type of our ideal,
At least my heart and prayer return to thee,
Amidst a faithless world of proselytes.
Madonna Mary, with her virgin lips,
And eyes that look perpetual reproach,
Insults and is a blasphemy on youth.

Is she to claim the worship of a man
Hot with the first rich flush of ripened life?'
Realities, like phantoms, glided by,
Unnoted 'midst the torment and delights
Of my conflicting spirit, and I doffed
the modest Christian weeds of charity
And fit humility, and steeled myself
In pagan panoply of stoicism
And self-sufficing pride. Yet constantly
I gained men's charmed attention and applause,
With the wild strains I smote from out my lyre,
To me the native language of my soul,
To them attractive and miraculous,
As all things whose solution and whose source
Remain a mystery. Then came suddenly
The summons to attend the gathering
Of minstrels at the Landgrave Hermann's court.
Resolved to publish there my pagan creed
In harmonies so high and beautiful
That all the world would share my zeal and faith,
I journeyed towards the haunted Horsel cliffs.
O God! how may I tell you how SHE came,
The temptress of a hundred centuries,
Yet fresh as April? She bewitched my sense,
Poisoned my judgment with sweet flatteries,
And for I may not guess how many years
Held me a captive in degrading bonds.
There is no sin of lust so lewd and foul,
Which I learned not in that alluring hell,
Until this morn, I snapped the ignoble tie,
By calling on the Mother of our Lord.
O for the power to stand again erect,
And look men in the eyes! What penitence,
What scourging of the flesh, what rigid fasts,
What terrible privations may suffice
To cleanse me in the sight of God and man?'
Ill-omened silence followed his appeal.
Patient and motionless he lay awhile,
Then sprang unto his feet with sudden force,
Confronting in his breathless vehemence,
With palpitating heart, the timid priest.
'Answer me, as you hope for a response,
One day, at the great judgment seat yourself.'
'I cannot answer,' said the timid priest,
'I have not understood.' 'Just God! is this
The curse Thou layest upon me? I outstrip
The sympathy and brotherhood of men,
So far removed is my experience
From their clean innocence. Inspire me,
Prompt me to words that bring me near to them!
Father,' in gentler accents he resumed,

'Thank Heaven at your every orison
That sin like mine you cannot apprehend.
More than the truth perchance I have confessed,
But I have sinned, and darkly, this is true;
And I have suffered, and am suffering now.
Is there no help in your great Christian creed
Of liberal charity, for such a one?'
'My son,' the priest replied, 'your speech distraught
Hath quite bewildered me. I fain would hope
That Christ's large charity can reach your sin,
But I know naught. I cannot but believe
That the enchantress who first tempted you
Must be the Evil one, your early doubt
Was the possession of your soul by him.
Travel across the mountain to the town,
The first cathedral town upon the road
That leads to Rome, a sage and reverend priest,
The Bishop Adrian, bides there. Say you have come
From his leal servant, Friar Lodovick;
He hath vast lore and great authority,
And may absolve you freely of your sin.'

Over the rolling hills, through summer fields,
By noisy villages and lonely lanes,
Through glowing days, when all the landscape stretched
Shimmering in the heat, a pilgrim fared
Towards the cathedral town. Sir Tannhauser
Had donned the mournful sackcloth, girt his loins
With a coarse rope that ate into his flesh,
Muffled a cowl about his shaven head,
Hung a great leaden cross around his neck;
And bearing in his hands a knotty staff,
With swollen, sandaled feet he held his course.
He snatched scant rest at twilight or at dawn,
When his forced travel was least difficult.
But most he journeyed when the sky, o'ercast,
Uprolled its threatening clouds of dusky blue,
And angry thunder grumbled through the hills,
And earth grew dark at noonday, till the flash
Of the thin lightning through the wide sky leapt.
And tumbling showers scoured along the plain.
Then folk who saw the pilgrim penitent,
Drenched, weird, and hastening as as to some strange doom,
Swore that the wandering Jew had crossed their land,
And the Lord Christ had sent the deadly bolt
Harmless upon his cursed, immortal head.
At length the hill-side city's spires and roofs,
With all its western windows smitten red
By a rich sunset, and with massive towers
Of its cathedral overtopping all,
greeted his sight. Some weary paces more,

And as the twilight deepened in the streets,
He stood within the minster. How serene,
In sculptured calm of centuries, it seemed!
How cool and spacious all the dim-lit aisles,
Still hazy with fumes of frankincense!
The vesper had been said, yet here and there
A wrinkled beldam, or mourner veiled,
Or burly burgher on the cold floor knelt,
And still the organist, with wandering hands,
Drew from the keys mysterious melodies,
And filled the church with flying waifs of song,
That with ethereal beauty moved the soul
To a more tender prayer and gentler faith
Than choral anthems and the solemn mass.
A thousand memories, sweet to bitterness,
Rushed on the knight and filled his eyes with tears;
Youth's blamelessness and faith forever lost,
The love of his neglected lyre, his art,
Revived by these aerial harmonies.
He was unworthy now to touch the strings,
Too base to stir men's soul to ecstasy
And high resolves, as in the days agone;
And yet, with all his spirit's earnestness,
He yearned to feel the lyre between his hands,
To utter all the trouble of his life
Unto the Muse who understands and helps.
Outworn with travel, soothed to drowsiness
By dying music and sweet-scented air,
His limbs relaxed, and sleep possessed his frame.
Auroral light the eastern oriels touched,
When with delicious sense of rest he woke,
Amidst the cast and silent empty aisles.
'God's peace hath fallen upon me in this place;
This is my Bethel; here I feel again
A holy calm, if not of innocence,
Yet purest after that, the calm serene
Of expiation and forgiveness.'
He spake, and passed with staff and wallet forth
Through the tall portal to the open square,
And turning, paused to look upon the pile.
The northern front against the crystal sky
Loomed dark and heavy, full of sombre shade,
With each projecting buttress, carven cross,
Gable and mullion, tipped with laughing light
By the slant sunbeams of the risen morn.
The noisy swallows wheeled above their nests,
Builded in hidden nooks about the porch.
No human life was stirring in the square,
Save now and then a rumbling market-team,
Fresh from the fields and farms without the town.
He knelt upon the broad cathedral steps,

And kissed the moistened stone, while overhead
The circling swallows sang, and all around
The mighty city lay asleep and still.

To stranger's ears must yet again be made
The terrible confession; yet again
A deathly chill, with something worse than fear,
Seized the knight's heart, who knew his every word
Widened the gulf between his kind and him.
The Bishop sat with pomp of mitred head,
In pride of proven virtue, hearkening to all
With cold, official apathy, nor made
A sign of pity nor encouragement.
The friar understood the pilgrim's grief,
The language of his eyes; his speech alone
Was alien to these kind, untutored ears.
But this was truly to be misconstrued,
To tear each palpitating word alive
From out the depths of his remorseful soul,
And have it weighed with the precision cool
And the nice logic of a reasoning mind.
This spiritual Father judged his crime
As the mad mischief of a reckless boy,
That call for strict, immediate punishment.
But Tannhauser, who felt himself a man,
Though base, yet fallen through passions and rare gifts
Of an exuberant nature rankly rich,
And knew his weary head was growing gray
With a life's terrible experience,
Found his old sense of proper worth revive;
But modestly he ended: 'Yet I felt,
O holy Father, in the church, this morn,
A strange security, a peace serene,
As though e'en yet the Lord regarded me
With merciful compassion; yea, as though
Even so vile a worm as I might work
Mine own salvation, through repentant prayers.'
'Presumptuous man, it is no easy task
To expiate such sin; a space of prayer
That deprecates the anger of the Lord,
A pilgrimage through pleasant summer lands,
May not atone for years of impious lust;
Thy heart hath lied to thee in offering hope.'
'Is there no hope on earth?' the pilgrim sighed.
'None through thy penance,' said the saintly man.
'Yet there may be through mediation, help.
There is a man who by a blameless life
Hath won the right to intercede with God.
No sins of his own flesh hath he to purge,
The Cardinal Filippo, he abides,
Within the Holy City. Seek him out;

This is my only counsel, through thyself
Can be no help and no forgiveness.'

How different from the buoyant joy of morn
Was this discouraged sense of lassitude,
The Bishop's words were ringing in his ears,
Measured and pitiless, and blent with these,
The memory of the goddess' last wild cry,
'ONCE BEING MINE, THOU ART FOREVER MINE.'
Was it the truth, despite his penitence,
And the dedication of his thought to God,
That still some portion of himself was hers,
Some lust survived, some criminal regret,
For her corrupted love? He searched his heart:
All was remorse, religious and sincere,
And yet her dreadful curse still haunted him;
For all men shunned him, and denied him help,
Knowing at once in looking on his face,
Ploughed with deep lines and prematurely old,
That he had struggled with some deadly fiend,
And that he was no longer kin to them.
Just past the outskirts of the town, he stopped,
To strengthen will and courage to proceed.
The storm had broken o'er the sultry streets,
But now the lessening clouds were flying east,
And though the gentle shower still wet his face,
The west was cloudless while the sun went down,
And the bright seven-colored arch stood forth,
Against the opposite dull gray. There was
A beauty in the mingled storm and peace,
Beyond clear sunshine, as the vast, green fields
Basked in soft light, though glistening yet with rain.
The roar of all the town was now a buzz
Less than the insects' drowsy murmuring
That whirred their gauzy wings around his head.
The breeze that follows on the sunsetting
Was blowing whiffs of bruised and dripping grass
Into the heated city. But he stood,
Disconsolate with thoughts of fate and sin,
Still wrestling with his soul to win it back
From her who claimed it to eternity.
Then on the delicate air there came to him
The intonation of the minster bells,
Chiming the vespers, musical and faint.
He knew not what of dear and beautiful
There was in those familiar peals, that spake
Of his first boyhood and his innocence,
Leading him back, with gracious influence,
To pleasant thoughts and tender memories,
And last, recalling the fair hour of hope
He passed that morning in the church. Again,

The glad assurance of God's boundless love
Filled all his being, and he rose serene,
And journeyed forward with a calm content.

Southward he wended, and the landscape took
A warmer tone, the sky a richer light.
The gardens of the graceful, festooned with hops,
With their slight tendrils binding pole to pole,
Gave place to orchards and the trellised grape,
The hedges were enwreathed with trailing vines,
With clustering, shapely bunches, 'midst the growth
Of tangled greenery. The elm and ash
Less frequent grew than cactus, cypresses,
And golden-fruited or large-blossomed trees.
The far hills took the hue of the dove's breast,
Veiled in gray mist of olive groves. No more
He passed dark, moated strongholds of grim knights,
But terraces with marble-paven steps,
With fountains leaping in the sunny air,
And hanging gardens full of sumptuous bloom.
Then cloisters guarded by their dead gray walls,
Where now and then a golden globe of fruit
Or full-flushed flower peered out upon the road,
Nodding against the stone, and where he heard
Sometimes the voices of the chanting monks,
Sometimes the laugh of children at their play,
Amidst the quaint, old gardens. But these sights
Were in the suburbs of the wealthy towns.
For many a day through wildernesses rank,
Or marshy, feverous meadow-lands he fared,
The fierce sun smiting his close-muffled head;
Or 'midst the Alpine gorges faced the storm,
That drave adown the gullies melted snow
And clattering boulders from the mountain-tops.
At times, between the mountains and the sea
Fair prospects opened, with the boundless stretch
Of restless, tideless water by his side,
And their long wash upon the yellow sand.
Beneath this generous sky the country-folk
Could lead a freer life, the fat, green fields
Offered rich pasturage, athwart the air
Rang tinkling cow-bells and the shepherds' pipes.
The knight met many a strolling troubadour,
Bearing his cithern, flute, or dulcimer;
And oft beneath some castle's balcony,
At night, he heard their mellow voices rise,
Blent with stringed instruments or tambourines,
Chanting some lay as natural as a bird's.
Then Nature stole with healthy influence
Into his thoughts; his love of beauty woke,
His Muse inspired dreams as in the past.

But after this came crueler remorse,
And he would tighten round his loins the rope,
And lie for hours beside some wayside cross,
And feel himself unworthy to enjoy
The splendid gift and privilege of life.
Then forth he hurried, spurred by his desire
To reach the City of the Seven Hills,
And gain his absolution. Some leagues more
Would bring him to the vast Campagna land,
When by a roadside well he paused to rest.
'T was noon, and reapers in the field hard by
Lay neath the trees upon the sun-scorched grass.
But from their midst one came towards the well,
Not trudging like a man forespent with toil,
But frisking like a child at holiday,
With light steps. The pilgrim watched him come,
And found him scarcely older than a child,
A large-mouthed earthen pitcher in his hand,
And a guitar upon his shoulder slung.
A wide straw hat threw all his face in shade,
But doffing this, to catch whatever breeze
Might stir among the branches, he disclosed
A charming head of rippled, auburn hair,
A frank, fair face, as lovely as a girls,
With great, soft eyes, as mild and grave as kine's.
Above his head he slipped the instrument,
And laid it with his hat upon the turf,
Lowered his pitcher down the well-head cool,
And drew it dripping upward, ere he saw
The watchful pilgrim, craving (as he thought)
The precious draught. 'Your pardon, holy sir,
Drink first,' he cried, 'before I take the jar
Unto my father in the reaping-field.'
Touched by the cordial kindness of the lad,
The pilgrim answered, 'Thanks, my thirst is quenched
From mine own palm.' The stranger deftly poised
The brimming pitcher on his head, and turned
Back to the reaping-folk, while Tannhauser
Looked after him across the sunny fields,
Clasping each hand about his waist to bear
The balanced pitcher; then, down glancing, found
The lad's guitar near by, and fell at once
To striking its tuned string with wandering hands,
And pensive eyes filled full of tender dreams.
'Yea, holy sir, it is a worthless thing,
And yet I love it, for I make it speak.'
The boy again stood by him and dispelled
His train of fantasies half sweet, half sad.
'That was not in my thought,' the knight replied.
'Its worth is more than rubies; whoso hath
The art to make this speak is raised thereby

Above all loneliness or grief or fear.'
More to himself than to the lad he spake,
Who, understanding not, stood doubtfully
At a loss for answer; but the knight went on:
'How came it in your hands, and who hath tuned
your voice to follow it.' 'I am unskilled,
Good father, but my mother smote its strings
To music rare.' Diverted from one theme,
Pleased with the winsome candor of the boy,
The knight encouraged him to confidence;
Then his own gift of minstrelsy revealed,
And told bright tales of his first wanderings,
When in lords' castles and kings' palaces
Men still made place for him, for in his land
The gift was rare and valued at its worth,
And brought great victory and sounding fame.
Thus, in retracing all his pleasant youth,
His suffering passed as though it had not been.
Wide-eyed and open-mouthed the boy gave ear,
His fair face flushing with the sudden thoughts
That went and came, then, as the pilgrim ceased,
Drew breath and spake: 'And where now is your lyre?'
The knight with both hands hid his changed, white face,
Crying aloud, 'Lost! lost! forever lost!'
Then, gathering strength, he bared his face again
Unto the frightened, wondering boy, and rose
With hasty fear. 'Ah, child, you bring me back
Unwitting to remembrance of my grief,
For which I donned eternal garb of woe;
And yet I owe you thanks for one sweet hour
Of healthy human intercourse and peace.
'T is not for me to tarry by the way.
Farewell!' The impetuous, remorseful boy,
Seeing sharp pain on that kind countenance,
Fell at his feet and cried, 'Forgive my words,
Witless but innocent, and leave me not
Without a blessing.' Moved unutterably,
The pilgrim kissed with trembling lips his head,
And muttered, 'At this moment would to God
That I were worthy!' Then waved wasted hands
Over the youth in act of blessing him,
But faltered, 'Cleanse me through his innocence,
O heavenly Father!' and with quickening steps
Hastened away upon the road to Rome.
The noon was past, the reapers drew broad swaths
With scythes sun-smitten 'midst the ripened crop.
Thin shadows of the afternoon slept soft
On the green meadows as the knight passed forth.

He trudged amidst the sea of poisonous flowers
On the Campagna's undulating plain,

With Rome, the many-steepled, many-towered,
Before him regnant on her throne of hills.
A thick blue cloud of haze o'erhung the town,
But the fast-sinking sun struck fiery light
From shining crosses, roofs, and flashing domes.
Across his path an arching bridge of stone
Was raised above a shrunken yellow stream,
Hurrying with the light on every wave
Towards the great town and outward to the sea.
Upon the bridge's crest he paused, and leaned
Against the barrier, throwing back his cowl,
And gazed upon the dull, unlovely flood
That was the Tiber. Quaggy banks lay bare,
Muddy and miry, glittering in the sun,
And myriad insects hovered o'er the reeds,
Whose lithe, moist tips by listless airs were stirred.
When the low sun had dropped behind the hills,
He found himself within the streets of Rome,
Walking as in a sleep, where naught seemed real.
The chattering hubbub of the market-place
Was over now; but voices smote his ear
Of garrulous citizens who jostled past.
Loud cries, gay laughter, snatches of sweet song,
The tinkling fountains set in gardens cool
About the pillared palaces, and blent
With trickling of the conduits in the squares,
The noisy teams within the narrow streets,
All these the stranger heard and did not hear,
While ringing bells pealed out above the town,
And calm gray twilight skies stretched over it.
Wide open stood the doors of every church,
And through the porches pressed a streaming throng.
Vague wonderment perplexed him, at the sight
Of broken columns raised to Jupiter
Beside the cross, immense cathedrals reared
Upon a dead faith's ruins; all the whirl
And eager bustle of the living town
Filling the storied streets, whose very stones
Were solemn monuments, and spake of death.
Although he wrestled with himself, the thought
Of that poor, past religion smote his heart
With a huge pity and deep sympathy,
Beyond the fervor which the Church inspired.
Where was the noble race who ruled the world,
Moulded of purest elements, and stuffed
With sternest virtues, every man a king,
Wearing the purple native in his heart?
These lounging beggars, stealthy monks and priests,
And womanish patricians filled their place.
Thus Tannhauser, still half an infidel,
Pagan through mind and Christian through the heart,

Fared thoughtfully with wandering, aimless steps,
Till in the dying glimmer of the day
He raised his eyes and found himself alone
Amid the ruined arches, broken shafts,
And huge arena of the Coliseum.
He did not see it as it was, dim-lit
By something less than day and more than night,
With wan reflections of the rising moon
Rather divined than seen on ivied walls,
And crumbled battlements, and topless columns
But by the light of all the ancient days,
Ringed with keen eager faces, living eyes,
Fixed on the circus with a savage joy,
Where brandished swords flashed white, and human blood
Streamed o'er the thirsty dust, and Death was king.
He started, shuddering, and drew breath to see
The foul pit choked with weeds and tumbled stones,
The cross raised midmost, and the peaceful moon
Shining o'er all; and fell upon his knees,
Restored to faith in one wise, loving God.
Day followed day, and still he bode in Rome,
Waiting his audience with the Cardinal,
And from the gates, on pretext frivolous,
Passed daily forth, his Eminency slept,
Again, his Eminency was fatigued
By tedious sessions of the Papal court,
And thus the patient pilgrim was referred
Unto a later hour. At last the page
Bore him a missive with Filippo's seal,
That in his name commended Tannhauser
Unto the Pope. The worn, discouraged knight
Read the brief scroll, then sadly forth again,
Along the bosky alleys of the park,
Passed to the glare and noise of summer streets.
'Good God!' he muttered, 'Thou hast ears for all,
And sendest help and comfort; yet these men,
Thy saintly ministers, must deck themselves
With arrogance, and from their large delight
In all the beauty of the beauteous earth,
And peace of indolent, untempted souls,
Deny the hungry outcast a bare word.'
Yet even as he nourished bitter thoughts,
He felt a depth of clear serenity,
Unruffled in his heart beneath it all.
No outward object now had farther power
To wound him there, for the brooding o'er those deeps
Of vast contrition was boundless hope.

Yet not to leave a human chance untried,
He sought the absolution of the Pope.
In a great hall with airy galleries,

Thronged with high dignitaries of the Church,
He took his seat amidst the humblest friars.
Through open windows came sweet garden smells,
Bright morning light, and twittered song of birds.
Around the hall flashed gold and sunlit gems,
And splendid wealth of color, white-stoled priests,
And scarlet cardinals, and bishops clad
In violet vestments, while beneath the shade
Of the high gallery huddled dusky shapes,
With faded, travel-tattered, sombre smocks,
And shaven heads, and girdles of coarse hemp;
Some, pilgrims penitent like Tannhauser;
Some, devotees to kiss the sacred feet.
The brassy blare of trumpets smote the air,
Shrill pipes and horns with swelling clamor came,
And through the doorway's wide-stretched tapestries
Passed the Pope's trumpeters and mace-bearers,
His vergers bearing slender silver wands,
Then mitred bishops, red-clad cardinals,
The stalwart Papal Guard with halberds raised,
And then, with white head crowned with gold ingemmed,
The vicar of the lowly Galilean,
Holding his pastoral rod of smooth-hewn wood,
With censer swung before and peacock fans
Waved constantly by pages, either side.
Attended thus, they bore him to his throne,
And priests and laymen fell upon their knees.
Then, after pause of brief and silent prayer,
The pilgrims singly through the hall defiled,
To kiss the borders of the papal skirts,
Smiting their foreheads on the paven stone;
Some silent, abject, some accusing them
Of venial sins in accents of remorse,
Craving his grace, and passing pardoned forth.
Sir Tannhauser came last, no need for him
To cry 'Peccavi,' and crook suppliant knees.
His gray head rather crushed than bowed, his face
Livid and wasted, his deep thoughtful eyes,
His tall gaunt form in those unseemly weeds,
Spake more than eloquence. His hollow voice
Brake silence, saying, 'I am Tannhauser.
For seven years I lived apart from men,
Within the Venusberg.' A horror seized
The assembled folk; some turbulently rose;
Some clamored, 'From the presence cast him forth!'
But the knight never ceased his steady gaze
Upon the Pope. At last, 'I have not spoken
To be condemned,' he said, 'by such as these.
Thou, spiritual Father, answer me.
Look thou upon me with the eyes of Christ.
Can I through expiation gain my shrift,

And work mine own redemption?' 'Insolent man!'
Thundered the outraged Pope, 'is this the tone
Wherewith thou dost parade thy loathsome sin?
Down on thy knees, and wallow on the earth!
Nay, rather go! there is no ray of hope,
No gleam, through cycles of eternity,
For the redemption of a soul like thine.
Yea, sooner shall my pastoral rod branch forth
In leaf and blossom, and green shoots of spring,
Than Christ will pardon thee.' And as he spoke,
He struck the rod upon the floor with force
That gave it entrance 'twixt two loosened tiles,
So that it stood, fast-rooted and alone.
The knight saw naught, he only heard his judge
Ring forth his curses, and the court cry out
'Anathema!' and loud, and blent therewith,
Derisive laughter in the very hall,
And a wild voice that thrilled through flesh and heart:
'ONCE BEING MINE, THOU ART FOREVER MINE!'
Half-mad he clasped both hands upon his brow,
Amidst the storm of voices, till they died,
And all was silence, save the reckless song
Of a young bird upon a twig without.
Then a defiant, ghastly face he raised,
And shrieked, ''T is false! I am no longer thine!'
And through the windows open to the park,
Rushed forth, beyond the sight and sound of men.

By church nor palace paused he, till he passed
All squares and streets, and crossed the bridge of stone,
And stood alone amidst the broad expanse
Of the Campagna, twinkling in the heat.
He knelt upon a knoll of turf, and snapped
The cord that held the cross about his neck,
And far from him the leaden burden flung.
'O God! I thank Thee, that my faith in Thee
Subsists at last, through all discouragements.
Between us must no type nor symbol stand,
No mediator, were he more divine
Than the incarnate Christ. All forms, all priests,
I part aside, and hold communion free
Beneath the empty sky of noon, with naught
Between my nothingness and thy high heavens
Spirit with spirit. O, have mercy, God!
Cleanse me from lust and bitterness and pride,
Have mercy in accordance with my faith.'
Long time he lay upon the scorching grass,
With his face buried in the tangled weeds.
Ah! who can tell the struggles of his soul
Against its demons in that sacred hour,
The solitude, the anguish, the remorse?

When shadows long and thin lay on the ground,
Shivering with fever, helpless he arose,
But with a face divine, ineffable,
Such as we dream the face of Israel,
When the Lord's wrestling angel, at gray dawn,
Blessed him, and disappeared.
Upon the marsh,
All night, he wandered, striving to emerge
From the wild, pathless plain, now limitless
And colorless beneath the risen moon;
Outstretching like a sea, with landmarks none,
Save broken aqueducts and parapets,
And ruined columns glinting 'neath the moon.
His dress was dank and clinging with the dew;
A thousand insects fluttered o'er his head,
With buzz and drone; unseen cicadas chirped
Among the long, rank grass, and far and near
The fire-flies flickered through the summer air.
Vague thoughts and gleams prophetic filled his brain.
'Ah, fool!' he mused, 'to look for help from men.
Had they the will to aid, they lack the power.
In mine own flesh and soul the sin had birth,
Through mine own anguish it must be atoned.
Our saviours are not saints and ministers,
But tear-strung women, children soft of heart,
Or fellow-sufferers, who, by some chance word,
Some glance of comfort, save us from despair.
These I have found, thank heaven! to strengthen trust
In mine own kind, when all the world grew dark.
Make me not proud in spirit, O my God!
Yea, in thy sight I am one mass of sin,
One black and foul corruption, yet I know
My frailty is exceeded by thy love.
Neither is this the slender straw of hope,
Whereto I, drowning, cling, but firm belief,
That fills my inmost soul with vast content.
As surely as the hollow faiths of old
Shriveled to dust before one ray of Truth,
So will these modern temples pass away,
Piled upon rotten doctrines, baseless forms,
And man will look in his own breast for help,
Yea, search for comfort his own inward reins,
Revere himself, and find the God within.
Patience and patience!' Through the sleepless night
He held such thoughts; at times before his eyes
Flashed glimpses of the Church that was to be,
Sublimely simple in the light serene
Of future ages; then the vision changed
To the Pope's hall, thronged with high priests, who hurled
Their curses on him. Staggering, he awoke
Unto the truth, and found himself alone,

Beneath the awful stars. When dawn's first chill
Crept though the shivering grass and heavy leaves,
Giddy and overcome, he fell and slept
Upon the dripping weeds, nor dreamed nor stirred,
Until the wide plain basked in noon's broad light.
He dragged his weary frame some paces more,
Unto a solitary herdsman's hut,
Which, in the vagueness of the moonlit night,
Was touched with lines of beauty, till it grew
Fair as the ruined works of ancient art,
Now squat and hideous with its wattled roof,
Decaying timbers, and loose door wide oped,
Half-fallen from the hinge. A drowsy man,
Bearded and burnt, in shepherd habit lay,
Stretched on the floor, slow-munching, half asleep,
His frugal fare; for thus, at blaze of noon,
The shepherds sought a shelter from the sun,
Leaving their vigilant dogs beside their flock.
The knight craved drink and bread, and with respect
For pilgrim weeds, the Roman herdsman stirred
His lazy length, and shared with him his meal.
Refreshed and calm, Sir Tannhauser passed forth,
Yearning with morbid fancy once again
To see the kind face of the minstrel boy
He met beside the well. At set of sun
He reached the place; the reaping-folk were gone,
The day's toil over, yet he took his seat.
A milking-girl with laden buckets full,
Came slowly from the pasture, paused and drank.
From a near cottage ran a ragged boy,
And filled his wooden pail, and to his home
Returned across the fields. A herdsman came,
And drank and gave his dog to drink, and passed,
Greeting the holy man who sat there still,
Awaiting. But his feeble pulse beat high
When he descried at last a youthful form,
Crossing the field, a pitcher on his head,
Advancing towards the well. Yea, this was he,
The same grave eyes, and open, girlish face.
But he saw not, amidst the landscape brown,
The knight's brown figure, who, to win his ear,
Asked the lad's name. 'My name is Salvator,
To serve you, sir,' he carelessly replied,
With eyes and hands intent upon his jar,
Brimming and bubbling. Then he cast one glance
Upon his questioner, and left the well,
Crying with keen and sudden sympathy,
'Good Father, pardon me, I knew you not.
Ah! you have travelled overmuch: your feet
Are grimed with mud and wet, your face is changed,
Your hands are dry with fever.' But the knight:

'Nay, as I look on thee, I think the Lord
Wills not that I should suffer any more.'
'Then you have suffered much,' sighed Salvator,
With wondering pity. 'You must come with me;
My father knows of you, I told him all.
A knight and minstrel who cast by his lyre,
His health and fame, to give himself to God,
Yours is a life indeed to be desired!
If you will lie with us this night, our home
Will verily be blessed.' By kindness crushed,
Wandering in sense and words, the broken knight
Resisted naught, and let himself be led
To the boy's home. The outcast and accursed
Was welcomed now by kindly human hands;
Once more his blighted spirit was revived
By contact with refreshing innocence.
There, when the morning broke upon the world,
The humble hosts no longer knew their guest.
His fleshly weeds of sin forever doffed,
Tannhauser lay and smiled, for in the night
The angel came who brings eternal peace.

Far into Wartburg, through all Italy,
In every town the Pope sent messengers,
Riding in furious haste; among them, one
Who bore a branch of dry wood burst in bloom;
The pastoral rod had borne green shoots of spring,
And leaf and blossom. God is merciful.

Lohengrin

The holy bell, untouched by human hands,
Clanged suddenly, and tolled with solemn knell.

Between the massive, blazoned temple-doors,
Thrown wide, to let the summer morning in,
Sir Lohengrin, the youngest of the knights,
Had paused to taste the sweetness of the air.
All sounds came up the mountain-side to him,
Softened to music, noise of laboring men,
The cheerful cock-crow and the low of kine,
Bleating of sheep, and twittering of the birds,
Commingled into murmurous harmonies
When harsh, and near, and clamorous tolled the bell.
He started, with his hand upon his sword;
His face, an instant since serene and fair,
And simple with the beauty of a boy,
Heroic, flushed, expectant all at once.

The lovely valley stretching out beneath
Was now a painted picture, nothing more;
All music of the mountain or the vale
Rang meaningless to him who heard the bell.
'I stand upon the threshold, and am called,'
His clear, young voice shrilled gladly through the air,
And backward through the sounding corridors.

'And have ye heard the bell, my brother knights,
Untouched by human hands or winds of heaven?
It called me, yea, it called my very name!'
So, breathing still of morning, Lohengrin
Sprang 'midst the gathering circle of the knights,
Eager, exalted. 'Nay, it called us all:
It rang as it hath often rung before,
Because the good cause, somewhere on the earth,
Requires a champion,' with a serious smile,
An older gravely answered. 'Where to go?
We know not, and we know not whom to serve.'
Then spake Sir Percivale, their holiest knight,
And father of the young Sir Lohengrin:
'All that to us seems old, familiar, stale,
Unto the boy is vision, miracle.
Cross him not, brethren, in his first desire.
I will dare swear the summons rang to him,
Not sternly solemn, as it tolled to us,
But gracious, sweet, and gay as marriage-bells.'
His pious hands above the young man's head
Wandered in blessing, lightly touching it,
As fondly as a mother. 'Lohengrin,
My son, farewell, God send thee faith and strength.'
'God send me patience and humility,'
Murmured the boyish knight, from contrite heart,
With head downcast for those anointing hands.
Then raising suddenly wide, innocent eyes,
'Father, my faith is boundless as God's love.'

Complete in glittering silver armor clad,
With silver maiden-shield, blank of device,
Sir Lohengrin rode down the Montsalvatsch,
With Percivale and Tristram, Frimutelle
And Eliduc, to speed him on his quest.
They fared in silence, for the elder knights
Were filled with grave misgivings, solemn thoughts
Of fate and sorrow, and they heard the bell
Tolling incessant; while Sir Lohengrin,
Buoyant with hope, and dreaming like a girl,
With wild blood dancing in his veins, had made
The journey down the mount unconsciously,
Surprised to find that he had reached the vale.
Distinct and bowered in green the mountain loomed,

Topped with the wondrous temple, with its cross
Smitten to splendor by the eastern sun.
Around them lay the valley beautiful,
Imparadised with flowers and light of June;
And through the valley flowed a willowy stream,
Golden and gray, at this delicious hour,
With purity and sunshine. Here the knights,
Irresolute, gave pause — which path to choose?
'God lead me right!' said meek Sir Lohengrin;
And as he spoke afar upon the stream,
He saw a shining swan approaching them.
Full-breasted, with the current it sailed down,
Dazzling in sun and shadow, air and wave,
With unseen movement, wings a little spread,
Their downy under-feathers fluttering,
Stirred by its stately progress; in its beak
It held a silver chain, and drew thereby
A dainty carven shallop after it,
Embossed with silver and with ivory.
'Lead ye my charger up the mount again,'
Cried Lohengrin, and leaped unto the ground,
'For I will trust my guidance to the swan.'
'Nay, hold, Sir Lohengrin,' said Eliduc,
'Thou hast not made provision for this quest.'
'God will provide,' the pious knight replied.
Then Percival: 'Be faithful to thy vows;
Bethink thee of thine oath when thou art asked
Thy mission in the temple, or thy race.
Farewell, farewell.' 'Farewell,' cried Lohengrin,
And sprang into the shallop as it passed,
And waved farewells unto his brother knights,
Until they saw the white and silver shine
Of boat and swan and armor less and less,
Till in the willowy distance they were lost.

Skirting the bases of the rolling hills,
He glided on the river hour by hour,
All through the endless summer day. At first
On either side the willows brushed his boat,
Then underneath their sweeping arch he passed,
Into a rich, enchanted wilderness,
Cool, full of mystic shadows and rare lights,
Wherein the very river changed its hue,
Reflecting tender shades of waving green,
And mossy undergrowth of grass and fern.
Here yellow lilies floated 'midst broad leaves,
Upon their reedy stalks, and far below,
Beneath the flags and rushes, coppery bream
Sedately sailed, and flickering perch, and dace
With silvery lustres caught the glancing rays
Of the June sun upon their mottled scales.

'Midst the close sedge the bright-eyed water-mouse
Nibbled its food, while overhead, its kin,
The squirrel, frisked among the trees. The air
Was full of life and sound of restless birds,
Darting with gayer tints of red and blue
And speckled plumage 'mid gray willow leaves,
And sober alders, and light-foliaged birch.
Unnumbered insects fluttered o'er the banks,
Some dimpling the smooth river's slippery floor,
Leaping from point to point. Then passed the knight
'Twixt broad fields basking in excess of light,
And girt around by range on range of hills,
Green, umber, purple, waving limitless,
Unto the radiant crystal of the sky.
Through unfamiliar solitudes the swan
Still led him, and he saw no living thing
Save creatures of the wood, no human face,
Nor sign of human dwelling. But he sailed,
Holding high thoughts and vowing valorous vows,
Filled with vast wonder and keen happiness,
At the world's very beauty, and his life
Opened in spacious vistas measureless,
As lovely as the stream that bore him on.
So dazzled was the boyish Lohengrin
By all the vital beauty of the real,
And the yet wilder beauty of his dreams,
That he had lost all sense of passing time,
And woke as from a trance of centuries,
To find himself within the heart of hills,
The river widened to an ample lake,
And the swan faring towards a narrow gorge,
That seemed to lead him to the sunset clouds.
Suffused with color were the extremest heights;
The river rippled in a glassy flood,
Glorying in the glory of the sky.
O what a moment for a man to take
Down with him in his memory to the grave!
Life at that hour appeared as infinite
As expectation, sacred, wonderful,
A vision and a privilege. The stream
Lessened to force its way through rocky walls,
Then swerved and flowed, a purple brook, through woods
Dewy with evening, sunless, odorous.
There Lohengrin, with eyes upon the stream,
Now brighter than the earth, saw, deep and clear,
The delicate splendor of the earliest star.
All night, too full of sweet expectancy,
Too reverent of the loveliness, for sleep,
He watched the rise and setting of the stars..
All things were new upon that magic day,
Suggesting nobler possibilities,

For a life passed in wise serenity,
Confided with sublimely simple faith
Unto the guidance of the higher will.
In the still heavens hung the large round moon,
White on the blue-black ripples glittering,
And rolled soft floods of slumberous, misty light
Over dim fields and colorless, huge hills.
But the pure swan still bore its burden on,
The ivory shallop and the silver knight,
Pale-faced in that white lustre, neither made
For any port, but seemed to float at will
Aimlessly in a strange, unpeopled land.
So passed the short fair night, and morning broke
Upon the river where it flowed through flats
Wide, fresh, and vague in gray, uncertain dawn,
With cool air sweet from leagues of dewy grass.
Then 'midst the flush and beauty of the east,
The risen sun made all the river flow,
Smitten with light, in gold and gray again.
Rightly he judged his voyage but begun,
When the swan loitered by low banks set thick
With cresses, and red berries, and sweet herbs,
That he might pluck and taste thereof; for these
Such wondrous vigor in his frame infused,
They seemed enchanted and ambrosial fruits.
Day waxed and waned and vanished many times,
And many suns still found him journeying;
But when the sixth night darkened hill and wold,
He seemed bewitched as by a wizard's spell,
By this slow, constant progress, and deep sleep
Possessed his spirit, and his head drooped low
On the hard pillow of his silver shield.
Unconscious he was borne through silent hours,
Nor wakened by the dawn of a new day,
But in his dreamless sleep he never lost
The sense of moving forward on a stream.
Now fared the swan through tilled and cultured lands,
Dappled with sheep and kine on pastures soft,
Sprinkled with trim and pleasant cottages,
With men and women working noiselessly,
As in a picture; nearer then they drew,
And sounds of rural labor, spoken words,
Sir Lohengrin might hear, but still he slept,
Nor saw the shining turrets of a town,
Gardens and castles, domes and cross-topped spires
Fair in the distance, and the flowing stream,
Cleaving its liquid path 'midst many men,
And glittering galleries filled with courtly folk,
Ranged for a tourney-show in open air.
Ah! what a miracle it seemed to these,
The white bird bearing on the river's breast

That curious, sparkling shallop, and within
The knight in silver armor, with bared head,
And crisp hair blown about his angel face,
Asleep upon his shield! They gazed on him
As on the incarnate spirit of pure faith,
And as the very ministrant of God.
But one great damsel throned beside a king,
With coroneted head and white, wan face,
Flushed suddenly, and clasped her hands in prayer,
And raised large, lucid eyes in thanks to Heaven.
Then, in his dreamless slumber, Lohengrin,
Feeling the steady motion of the boat
Suddenly cease, awoke. Refreshed, alert,
He knew at once that he had reached his port,
And saw that peerless maiden thanking Heaven
For his own advent, and his heart leaped up
Into his throat, and love o'ermastered him.
After the blare of flourished trumpets died,
A herald thus proclaimed the tournament:
'Greetings and glory to the majesty
Of the imperial Henry. By his grace,
This tourney has been granted to the knight,
Frederick of Telramund, who claims the hand
Of Lady Elsie, Duchess of Brabant,
His ward, and stands prepared to prove in arms
His rights against all champions in the lists,
Whom his unwilling mistress may select.
Sir Frederick, Lord of Telramund, is here:
What champion will espouse the lady's cause?'
Sir Frederick, huge in stature and in bulk,
In gleaming armor terribly equipped,
Advanced defiant, as the herald ceased.
Then Lohengrin, with spear and shield in hand,
Sprang lightly, from his shallop, in the lists.
His beaver raised disclosed his ardent face,
His whole soul shining from inspired eyes.
With cast-back head, sun-smitten silver mail,
Quivering with spirit, light, and life, he stood,
And flung his gauntlet at Sir Frederick's feet,
Crying with shrill, clear voice that rang again,
'Sir Lohengrin adopts the lady's cause.'
Then these with shock of conflict couched their spears
In deadly combat; but their weapons clanged
Harmless against their mail impregnable,
Or else were nimbly foiled by dexterous shields.
Unequal and unjust it seemed at first,
The slender boy matched with the warrior huge,
Who bore upon him with the skill and strength
Of a tried conqueror; but the stranger knight
Displayed such agile grace in parrying blows,
Such fiery valor dealing his own strokes,

That men looked on in wonder, and his foe
Was hardly put upon it for his life.
Thrice they gave praise, to breathe, and to prepare
For fiercer battle, and the galleries rang
With plaudits, and the names of both the knights.
And they, with spirits whetted by the strife,
Met for the fourth, last time, and fenced and struck,
And the keen lance of Lohengrin made way,
Between the meshes of Sir Frederick's mail,
Through cuirass and through jerkin, to the flesh,
With pain so sharp and sudden that he fell.
Then Henry threw his warder to the ground,
And cried the stranger knight had won the day;
And all the lesser voices, following his,
Called, 'Lohengrin—Sir Lohengrin hath won!'
He, flushed with victory, standing in the lists,
Deafened with clamor of his very name,
Reëchoed to the heavens, felt himself
Alone and alien, and would fain float back
Unto the temple, had he not recalled
The fair, great damsel throned beside the king.
But lo! the swan had vanished, and the boat
He fancied he descried a tiny star,
Glimmering in the shining distances.
'His Majesty would greet Sir Lohengrin;
And Lady Elsie, Duchess of Brabant,
Would thank him for his prowess.' Thus proclaimed
The herald, while the unknown knight was led
To the imperial throne. Then Elsie spake:
'Thou hast redeemed my life from misery;
How may I worthily reward or thank?
Be thou the nearest to our ducal throne,
The highest knight of Limburg and Brabant,
The greatest gentleman, unless thy rank,
In truth, be suited to thine own deserts,
And thou, a prince, art called to higher aims.'
'Madam, my thanks are rather due to Fate,
For having chosen so poor an instrument
For such a noble end. A knight am I,
The champion of the helpless and oppressed,
Bound by fast vows to own no other name
Than Lohengrin, the Stranger, in this land,
And to depart when asked my race or rank.
Trusting in God I came, and, trusting Him,
I must remain, for all my fate hath changed,
All my desires and hopes, since I am here.'

So ended that great joust, and in the days
Thereafter Elsie and Sir Lohengrin,
United by a circumstance so strange,
Loved and were wedded. A more courteous duke,

A braver chevalier, Brabant ne'er saw.
Such grace breathed from his person and his deeds,
Such simple innocence and faith looked forth
From eyes well-nigh too beautiful for man,
That whom he met, departed as his friend.
But Elsie, bound to him by every bond
Of love and honor and vast gratitude,
Being of lesser faith and confidence,
Tortured herself with envious jealousies,
Misdoubting her own beauty, and her power
To win and to retain so great a heart.
Each year Sir Lohengrin proclaimed a joust
In memory of the tourney where he won
His lovely Duchess, and his lance prevailed
Against all lesser knights. When his twain sons,
Loyal and brave and gentle as their sire,
Had grown to stalwart men, and his one girl,
Eyed like himself and as his Duchess fair,
Floramie, grew to gracious maidenhood,
He gave a noble tourney, and o'erthrew
The terrible and potent Duke of Cleves.
'Ha!' sneered the Dame of Cleves, 'this Lohengrin
May be a knight adroit and valorous,
But who knows whence he sprang?' and lightly laughed,
Seeing the hot blood kindle Elsie's cheek.
That night Sir Lohengrin sought rest betimes,
By hours of crowded action quite forespent,
And found the Duchess Elsie on her couch,
Staining the silken broideries with her tears.
'Why dost thou weep?' he questioned tenderly,
Kissing her delicate hands, and parting back
Her heavy yellow hair from brow and face.
'The Duchess Anne of Cleves hath wounded me.'
'Sweet, am not I at hand to comfort thee?'
And he caressed her as an ailing child,
Until she smiled and slept. But the next night
He found her weeping, and he questioned her,
With the same answer, and again she slept;
Then the third night he asked her why she grieved
And she uprising, white, with eager eyes,
Cried, 'Lohengrin, my lord, my only love,
For our sons' sake, who know not whence they spring,
Our daughter who remains a virgin yet,
Let me not hear folk girding at thy race.
I know thy blood is royal, I have faith;
But tell me all, that I may publish it
Unto our dukedom.' Hurt and wondering,
He answered simply, 'I am Lohengrin,
Son to Sir Percivale, and ministrant
Within the holy temple of the Grail.
I would thy faith were greater, this is all.

Now must I bid farewell.' 'O Lohengrin,
What have I done?' She clung about his neck,
And moistened all his beard with streaming tears;
But he with one long kiss relaxed her arms
Calmly from his embrace, and stood alone.
' Blame not thy nature now with vain reproofs.
This also is our fate: in all things else.
We have submitted,let us yield in this,
With no less grace now that God tries our hearts,
Than when He sent us victory and love.'
' Yea, go, you never loved me,' faltered she;
' I will not blame my nature, but your own.
Through all our wedded years I doubted you;
Your eyes have never brightened meeting mine
As I have seen them in religious zeal,
Or in exalted hours of victory.'
A look of perfect weariness, unmixed
With wrath or grief, o'erspread the knight's pale face;
But with the pity that a god might show
Towards one with ills impossible to him,
He drew anear, caressing her, and sighed:
' Through all our wedded years you doubted me?
Poor child, poor child! and it has come to this.
Thank Heaven, I gave no cause for your mistrust,
Desiring never an ideal more fair
Of womanhood than was my chosen wife.'
She, broken, sobbing, leaned her delicate head
On his great shoulder, and remorseful cried,
' O loyal, honest, simple Lohengrin,
Thy wife has been unworthy: this is why
Thou sayest farewell in accents cold and strange,
With alien eyes that even now behold
Things fairer, better, than her mournful face.'
But he with large allowance answered her:
'If this be truth, it is because I feel
That I belong no more unto myself,
Neither to thee, for God withdraws my soul
Beyond all earthly passions unto Him.
Now that we know our doom, with serious calm,
Beside thee I will sit, till break of day,
Thus holding thy chill hand and tell thee all.
This will resign thee, for I cannot think
How any human soul that hath beheld
Life's compensations and its miracles,
Can fail to trust in what is yet to come.'
Then he began from that auroral hour
When he first heard the temple bell, and told
The wonder of the swan that came for him,
His journey down the stream, the tournament,
His strength unwonted, combating the knight
Who towered above him with superior force

Of flesh and sinew, how he prayed through all,
Imploring God to let the just cause win,
Unconscious of the close-thronged galleries,
Feeling two eyes alone that burned his soul.
She knew the rest. Therewith he kissed her brow
And ended, 'Now the knights will take me back
Into the temple; all who keep their vows,
Are welcomed there again to peace and rest.
There will my years fall from me like a cloak,
And I will stand again at manhood's prime.
Then when all errors of the flesh are purged
From these I loved here, they may follow me,
Unto perpetual worship and to peace.'
She lay quite calm, and smiling heard his voice,
Already grown to her remote and changed,
And when he ceased, arose and gazed in awe
On his transfigured face and kissed his brow,
And understood, accepting all her fate.
Anon he called his children, and to these:
'Farewell, sweet Florance and dear Percivale;
Here is my horn, and here mine ancient sword,
Guard them with care and win with them repute.
Here, Elsie, is the ring my mother gave,
Part with it never; and thou, Floramie,
Take thou my love, I have naught else to give;
Be of strong faith in him thou mean'st to wed.'
So these communed together, till the night
Died from the brightening skies, and in the east
The morning star hung in aerial rose,
And the blue deepened; while moist lawn and hedge
Breathed dewy freshness through the windows oped.
Then on the stream, that nigh the palace flowed,
A stainless swan approached them; in its beak
It held a silver chain, and drew thereby
A dainty, carven shallop after it,
Embossed with silver and with ivory.
Followed by waved farewells and streaming eyes,
Sir Lohengrin embarked and floated forth
Unto perpetual worship and to peace.

Phantasies

I. Evening

Rest, beauty, stillness: not a waif of a cloud
From gray-blue east sheer to the yellow west
No film of mist the utmost slopes to shroud.

The earth lies grace, by quiet airs caressed,

And shepherdeth her shadows, but each stream,
Free to the sky, is by that glow possessed,
And traileth with the splendors of a dream
Athwart the dusky land. Uplift thine eyes!
Unbroken by a vapor or a gleam,

The vast clear reach of mild, wan twilight skies.
But look again, and lo, the evening star!
Against the pale tints black the slim elms rise,

The earth exhales sweet odors nigh and far,
And from the heavens fine influences fall.
Familiar things stand not for what they are:

What they suggest, foreshadow, or recall
The spirit is alert to apprehend,
Imparting somewhat of herself to all.

Labor and thought and care are at an end:
The soul is filled with gracious reveries,
And with her mood soft sounds and colors blend;

For simplest sounds ring forth like melodies
In this weird-lighted air the monotone
Of some far bell, the distant farmyard cries,

A barking dog, the thin, persistent drone
Of crickets, and the lessening call of birds.
The apparition of yon star alone

Breaks on the sense like music. Beyond word
The peace that floods the soul, for night is here,
And Beauty still is guide and harbinger.

II. Aspiration

Dark lies the earth, and bright with worlds the sky:
That soft, large, lustrous star, that first outshone,
Still holds us spelled with potent sorcery.

Dilating, shrinking, lightening, it hath won
Our spirit with its strange strong influence,
And sways it as the tides beneath the moon.

What impulse this, o'ermastering heart and sense?
Exalted, thrilled, the freed soul fain would soar
Unto that point of shining prominence,

Craving new fields and some unheard-of shore,
Yea, all the heavens, for her activity,

To mount with daring flight, to hover o'er

Low hills of earth, flat meadows, level sea,
And earthly joy and trouble. In this hour
Of waning light and sound, of mystery,

Of shadowed love and beauty-veiled power,
She feels her wings: she yearns to grasp her own,
Knowing the utmost good to be her dower.

A dream! a dream! for at a touch 't is gone.
O mocking spirit! thy mere fools are we,
Unto the depths from heights celestial thrown.

From these blind gropings toward reality,
This thirst for truth, this most pathetic need
Of something to uplift, to justify,

To help and comfort while we faint and bleed,
May we not draw, wrung from the last despair,
Some argument of hope, some blessed creed,

That we can trust the faith which whispers prayer,
The vanishings, the ecstasy, the gleam,
The nameless aspiration, and the dream?

III. Wherefore?

Deep languor overcometh mind and frame:
A listless, drowsy, utter weariness,
A trance wherein no thought finds speech or name,

The overstrained spirit doth possess.
She sinks with drooping wing-poor unfledged bird,
That fain had flown! in fluttering breathlessness.

To what end those high hopes that wildly stirred
The beating heart with aspirations vain?
Why proffer prayers unanswered and unheard

To blank, deaf heavens that will not heed her pain?
Where lead these lofty, soaring tendencies,
That leap and fly and poise, to fall again,

Yet seem to link her with the utmost skies?
What mean these clinging loves that bind to earth,
And claim her with beseeching, wistful eyes?

This little resting-place 'twixt death and birth,
Why is it fretted with the ceaseless flow

Of flood and ebb, with overgrowth and dearth,

And vext with dreams, and clouded with strange woe?
Ah! she is tired of thought, she yearns for peace,
Seeing all things one equal end must know.

Wherefore this tangle of perplexities,
The trouble or the joy? the weary maze
Of narrow fears and hopes that may not cease?

A chill falls on her from the skyey ways,
Black with the night-tide, where is none to hear
The ancient cry, the Wherefore of our days.

IV. Fancies

The ceaseless whirr of crickets fills the ear
From underneath each hedge and bush and tree,
Deep in the dew-drenched grasses everywhere.

The simple sound dispels the fantasy
Of gloom and terror gathering round the mind.
It seems a pleasant thing to breathe, to be,

To hear the many-voiced, soft summer wind
Lisp through the dark thick leafage overhead
To see the rosy half-moon soar behind

The black slim-branching elms. Sad thoughts have fled,
Trouble and doubt, and now strange reveries
And odd caprices fill us in their stead.

From yonder broken disk the redness dies,
Like gold fruit through the leaves the half-sphere gleams,
Then over the hoar tree-tops climbs the skies,

Blanched ever more and more, until it beams
Whiter than crystal. Like a scroll unfurled,
And shadowy as a landscape seen in dreams,

Reveals itself the sleeping, quiet world,
Painted in tender grays and whites subdued
The speckled stream with flakes of light impearled,

The wide, soft meadow and the massive wood.
Naught is too wild for our credulity
In this weird hour: our finest dreams hold good.

Quaint elves and frolic flower-sprites we see,
And fairies weaving rings of gossamer,

And angels floating through the filmy air.

V. In the Night

Let us go in: the air is dank and chill
With dewy midnight, and the moon rides high
O'er ghostly fields, pale stream, and spectral hill.

This hour the dawn seems farthest from the sky
So weary long the space that lies between
That sacred joy and this dark mystery

Of earth and heaven: no glimmering is seen,
In the star-sprinkled east, of coming day,
Nor, westward, of the splendor that hath been.

Strange fears beset us, nameless terrors sway
The brooding soul, that hungers for her rest,
Out worn with changing moods, vain hopes' delay,

With conscious thought o'erburdened and oppressed.
The mystery and the shadow wax too deep;
She longs to merge both sense and thought in sleep.

VI. Faerie

From the oped lattice glance once more abroad
While the ethereal moontide bathes with light
Hill, stream, and garden, and white-winding road.

All gracious myths born of the shadowy night
Recur, and hover in fantastic guise,
Airy and vague, before the drowsy sight.

On yonder soft gray hill Endymion lies
In rosy slumber, and the moonlit air
Breathes kisses on his cheeks and lips and eyes.

'Twixt bush and bush gleam flower-white limbs, left bare,
Of huntress-nymphs, and flying raiment thin,
Vanishing faces, and bright floating hair.

The quaint midsummer fairies and their kin,
Gnomes, elves, and trolls, on blossom, branch, and grass
Gambol and dance, and winding out and in

Leave circles of spun dew where'er they pass.
Through the blue ether the freed Ariel flies;
Enchantment holds the air; a swarming mass

Of myriad dusky, gold-winged dreams arise,
Throng toward the gates of sense, and so possess
The soul, and lull it to forgetfulness.

VII. Confused Dreams

O strange, dim other-world revealed to us,
Beginning there where ends reality,
Lying 'twixt life and death, and populous

With souls from either sphere! now enter we
Thy twisted paths. Barred is the silver gate,
But the wild-carven doors of ivory

Spring noiselessly apart: between them straight
Flies forth a cloud of nameless shadowy things,
With harpies, imps, and monsters, small and great,

Blurring the thick air with darkening wings.
All humors of the blood and brain take shape,
And fright us with our own imaginings.

A trouble weighs upon us: no escape
From this unnatural region can there be.
Fixed eyes stare on us, wide mouths grin and gape,

Familiar faces out of reach we see.
Fain would we scream, to shatter with a cry
The tangled woof of hideous fantasy,

When, lo! the air grows clear, a soft fair sky
Shines over head: sharp pain dissolves in peace;
Beneath the silver archway quietly

We float away: all troublous visions cease.
By a strange sense of joy we are possessed,
Body and spirit soothed in perfect rest.

VIII. The End of the Song

What dainty note of long-drawn melody
Athwart our dreamless sleep rings sweet and clear,
Till all the fumes of slumber are brushed by,

And with awakened consciousness we hear
The pipe of birds? Look forth! The sane, white day
Blesses the hilltops, and the sun is near.

All misty phantoms slowly roll away
With the night's vapors toward the western sky.
The Real enchants us, the fresh breath of hay

Blows toward us; soft the meadow-grasses lie,
Bearded with dew; the air is a caress;
The sudden sun o'ertops the boundary

Of eastern hills, the morning joyousness
Thrills tingling through the frame; life's pulse beats strong;
Night's fancies melt like dew. So ends the song!

Raschi In Prague

Raschi of Troyes, the Moon of Israel,
The authoritative Talmudist, returned
From his wide wanderings under many skies,
To all the synagogues of the Orient,
Through Spain and Italy, the isles of Greece,
Beautiful, dolorous, sacred Palestine,
Dead, obelisked Egypt, floral, musk-breathed Persia,
Laughing with bloom, across the Caucasus,
The interminable sameness of bare steppes,
Through dark luxuriance of Bohemian woods,
And issuing on the broad, bright Moldau vale,
Entered the gates of Prague. Here, too, his fame,
Being winged, preceded him. His people swarmed
Like bees to gather the rich honey-dew
Of learning from his lips. Amazement filled
All eyes beholding him. No hoary sage,
He who had sat in Egypt at the feet
Of Moses ben-Maimuni, called him friend;
Raschi the scholiast, poet, and physician,
Who bore the ponderous Bible's storied wisdom,
The Mischna's tangled lore at tip of tongue,
Light as a garland on a lance, appeared
In the just-ripened glory of a man.
From his clear eye youth flamed magnificent;
Force, masked by grace, moved in his balanced frame;
An intellectual, virile beauty reigned
Dominant on domed brow, on fine, firm lips,
An eagle profile cut in gilded bronze,
Strong, delicate as a head upon a coin,
While, as an aureole crowns a burning lamp,
Above all beauty of the body and brain
Shone beauty of a soul benign with love.
Even as a tawny flock of huddled sheep,
Grazing each other's heels, urged by one will,
With bleat and baa following the wether's lead,

Or the wise shepherd, so o'er the Moldau bridge
Trotted the throng of yellow-caftaned Jews,
Chattering, hustling, shuffling. At their head
Marched Rabbi Jochanan ben-Eleazar,
High priest in Prague, oldest and most revered,
To greet the star of Israel. As a father
Yearns toward his son, so toward the noble Raschi
Leapt at first sight the patriarch's fresh old heart.
'My home be thine in Prague! Be thou my son,
Who have no offspring save one simple girl.
See, glorious youth, who dost renew the days
Of David and of Samuel, early graced
With God's anointing oil, how Israel
Delights to honor who hath honored him.'
Then Raschi, though he felt a ball of fire
Globe itself in his throat, maintained his calm,
His cheek's opaque, swart pallor while he kissed
Silent the Rabbi's withered hand, and bowed
Divinely humble, his exalted head
Craving the benison.
For each who asked
He had the word of counsel, comfort, help;
For all, rich eloquence of thanks. His voice,
Even and grave, thrilled secret chords and set
Plain speech to music. Certain folk were there
Sick in the body, dragging painful limbs,
To the physician. These he solaced first,
With healing touch, with simples from his pouch,
Warming and lulling, best with promises
Of constant service till their ills were cured.
And some, gray-bearded, bald, and curved with age,
Blear-eyed from poring over lines obscure
And knotty riddles of the Talmud, brought
Their problems to this youth, who cleared and solved,
Yielding prompt answer to a lifetime's search.
Then, followed, pushed by his obsequious tribe,
Who fain had pedestaled him on their backs,
Hemming his steps, choking the airs of heaven
With their oppressive honors, he advanced,
Midst shouts, tumultuous welcomes, kisses showered
Upon his road-stained garments, through Prague's streets,
Gaped at by Gentiles, hissed at and reviled,
But no whit altering his majestic mien
For overwhelming plaudits or contempt.
Glad tidings Raschi brought from West and East
Of thriving synagogues, of famous men,
And flourishing academies. In Rome
The Papal treasurer was a pious Jew,
Rabbi Jehiel, neath whose patronage
Prospered a noble school. Two hundred Jews
Dwelt free and paid no tributary mark.

Three hundred lived in peace at Capua,
Shepherded by the learned Rabbi David,
A prince of Israel. In Babylon
The Jews established their Academy.
Another still in Bagdad, from whose chair
Preached the great rabbi, Samuel Ha-levi,
Versed in the written and the oral law,
Who blindfold could repeat the whole vast text
Of Mischna and Gemara. On the banks
Of Eden born Euphrates, one day's ride
From Bagdad, Raschi found in the wilderness,
Which once was Babylon, Ezekiel's tomb.
Thrice ten perpetual lamps starred the dim shrine,
Two hundred sentinels held the sleepless vigil,
Receiving offerings. At the Feast of Booths
Here crowded Jews by thousands, out of Persia,
From all the neighboring lands, to celebrate
The glorious memories of the golden days.
Ten thousand Jews with their Academy
Damascus boasted, while in Cairo shone
The pearl, the crown of Israel, ben-Maimuni,
Physician at the Court of Saladin,
The second Moses, gathering at his feet
Sages from all the world.
As Raschi spake,
Forgetting or ignoring the chief shrine,
The Exile's Home, whereunto yearned all hearts,
All ears were strained for tidings. Some one asked:
'What of Jerusalem? Speak to us of Zion.'
The light died from his eyes. From depths profound
Issued his grave, great voice: 'Alas for Zion!
Verily is she fallen! Where our race
Dictated to the nations, not a handful,
Nay, not a score, not ten, not two abide!
One, only one, one solitary Jew,
The Rabbi Abraham Haceba, flits
Ghostlike amid the ruins; every year
Beggars himself to pay the idolaters
The costly tax for leave to hold a-gape
His heart's live wound; to weep, a mendicant,
Amidst the crumbled stones of palaces
Where reigned his ancestors, upon the graves
Where sleep the priests, the prophets, and the kings
Who were his forefathers. Ask me no more!'

Now, when the French Jew's advent was proclaimed,
And his tumultuous greeting, envious growls
And ominous eyebeams threatened storm in Prague.
'Who may this miracle of learning be?
The Anti-Christ! The century-long-awaited,
The hourly-hoped Messiah, come at last!

Else dared they never wax so arrogant,
Flaunting their monstrous joy in Christian eyes,
And strutting peacock-like, with hideous screams,
Who are wont to crawl, mute reptiles underfoot.'
A stone or two flung at some servile form,
Liveried in the yellow gaberdine
(With secret happiness but half suppressed
On features cast for misery), served at first
For chance expression of the rabble's hate;
But, swelling like a snow-ball rolled along
By mischief-plotting boys, the rage increased,
Grew to a mighty mass, until it reached
The palace of Duke Vladislaw. He heard
With righteous wrath his injured subjects' charge
Against presumptuous aliens: how these blocked
His avenues, his bridges; bared to the sun
The canker-taint of Prague's obscurest coigne;
Paraded past the churches of the Lord
One who denied Him, one by them hailed Christ.
Enough! This cloud, no bigger than one's hand,
Gains overweening bulk. Prague harbored, first,
Out of contemptuous ruth, a wretched band
Of outcast paupers, gave them leave to ply
Their money-lending trade, and leased them land
On all too facile terms. Behold! to-day,
Like leeches bloated with the people's blood,
They batten on Bohemia's poverty;
They breed and grow; like adders, spit back hate
And venomed perfidy for Christian love.
Thereat the Duke, urged by wise counsellors
Narzerad the statesman (half whose wealth was pledged
To the usurers), abetted by the priest,
Bishop of Olmutz, who had visited
The Holy Sepulchre, whose long, full life
Was one clean record of pure piety
The Duke, I say, by these persuasive tongues,
Coaxed to his darling aim, forbade his guards
To hinder the just anger of his town,
And ordered to be led in chains to him
The pilgrim and his host.

At noontide meal
Raschi sat, full of peace, with Jochanan,
And the sole daughter of the house, Rebekah,
Young, beautiful as her namesake when she brought
Her firm, frail pitcher balanced on her neck
Unto the well, and gave the stranger drink,
And gave his camels drink. The servant set
The sparkling jar's refreshment from his lips,
And saw the virgin's face, bright as the moon,
Beam from the curled luxuriance of black locks,

And cast-back linen veil's soft-folded cloud,
Then put the golden ear-ring by her cheek,
The bracelets on her hands, his master's pledge,
Isaac's betrothal gift, whom she should wed,
And be the mother of millions one whose seed
Dwells in the gates of those which hate them.
So
Yearned Raschi to adorn the radiant girl
Who sat at board before him, nor dared lift
Shy, heavy lids from pupils black as grapes
That dart the imprisoned sunshine from their core.
But in her ears keen sense was born to catch,
And in her heart strange power to hold, each tone
O' the low-keyed, vibrant voice, each syllable
O' the eloquent discourse, enriched with tales
Of venturous travel, brilliant with fine points
Of delicate humor, or illustrated
With living portraits of world-famoused men,
Jews, Saracens, Crusaders, Islamites,
Whose hand he had grasped the iron warrior,
Godfrey of Bouillon, the wise infidel
Who in all strength, wit, courtesy excelled
The kings his foes imperial Saladin.
But even as Raschi spake an abrupt noise
Of angry shouts, of battering staves that shook
The oaken portal, stopped the enchanted voice,
The uplifted wine spilled from the nerveless hand
Of Rabbi Jochanan. 'God pity us!
Our enemies are upon us once again.
Hie thee, Rebekah, to the inmost chamber,
Far from their wanton eyes' polluting gaze,
Their desecrating touch! Kiss me! Begone!
Raschi, my guest, my son' But no word more
Uttered the reverend man. With one huge crash
The strong doors split asunder, pouring in
A stream of soldiers, ruffians, armed with pikes,
Lances, and clubs the unchained beast, the mob.
'Behold the town's new guest!' jeered one who tossed
The half-filled golden wine-cup's contents straight
In the noble pure young face. 'What, master Jew!
Must your good friends of Prague break bolts and bars
To gain a peep at this prodigious pearl
You bury in your shell? Forth to the day!
Our Duke himself claims share of your new wealth;
Summons to court the Jew philosopher!'
Then, while some stuffed their pokes with baubles snatched
From board and shelf, or with malignant sword
Slashed the rich Orient rugs, the pictured woof
That clothed the wall; others had seized and bound,
And gagged from speech, the helpless, aged man;
Still others outraged, with coarse, violent hands,

The marble-pale, rigid as stone, strange youth,
Whose eye like struck flint flashed, whose nether lip
Was threaded with a scarlet line of blood,
Where the compressed teeth fixed it to forced calm.
He struggled not while his free limbs were tied,
His beard plucked, torn and spat upon his robe
Seemed scarce to know these insults were for him;
But never swerved his gaze from Jochanan.
Then, in God's language, sealed from these dumb brutes,
Swiftly and low he spake: 'Be of good cheer,
Reverend old man. I deign not treat with these.
If one dare offer bodily hurt to thee,
By the ineffable Name! I snap my chains
Like gossamer, and in his blood, to the hilt,
Bathe the prompt knife hid in my girdle's folds.
The Duke shall hear me. Patience. Trust in me.'
Somewhat the authoritative voice abashed,
Even hoarse and changed, the miscreants, who feared
Some strong curse lurked in this mysterious tongue,
Armed with this evil eye. But brief the spell.
With gibe and scoff they dragged their victims forth,
The abused old man, the proud, insulted youth,
O'er the late path of his triumphal march,
Befouled with mud, with raiment torn, wild hair
And ragged beard, to Vladislaw. He sat
Expectant in his cabinet. On one side
His secular adviser, Narzerad,
Quick-eyed, sharp-nosed, red-whiskered as a fox;
On the other hand his spiritual guide,
Bishop of Olmutz, unctuous, large, and bland.
'So these twain are chief culprits!' sneered the Duke,
Measuring with the noble's ignorant scorn
His masters of a lesser caste. 'Stand forth!
Rash, stubborn, vain old man, whose impudence
Hath choked the public highways with thy brood
Of nasty vermin, by our sufferance hid
In lanes obscure, who hailed this charlatan
With sky-flung caps, bent knees, and echoing shouts,
Due to ourselves alone in Prague; yea, worse,
Who offered worship even ourselves disclaim,
Our Lord Christ's meed, to this blaspheming Jew
Thy crimes have murdered patience. Thou hast wrecked
Thy people's fortune with thy own. But first
(For even in anger we are just) recount
With how great compensation from thy store
Of hoarded gold and jewels thou wilt buy
Remission of the penalty. Be wise.
Hark how my subjects, storming through the streets,
Vent on thy tribe accursed their well-based wrath.'
And, truly, through closed casements roared the noise
Of mighty surging crowds, derisive cries,

And victims' screams of anguish and affright.
Then Raschi, royal in his rags, began:
'Hear me, my liege!' At that commanding voice,
The Bishop, who with dazed eyes had perused
The grieved, wise, beautiful, pale face, sprang up,
Quick recognition in his glance, warm joy
Aflame on his broad cheeks. 'No more! No more!
Thou art the man! Give me the hand to kiss
That raised me from the shadow of the grave
In Jaffa's lazar-house! Listen, my liege!
During my pilgrimage to Palestine
I, sickened with the plague and nigh to death,
Languished 'midst strangers, all my crumbling flesh
One rotten mass of sores, a thing for dogs
To shy from, shunned by Christian as by Turk,
When lo! this clean-breathed, pure-souled, blessed youth,
Whom I, not knowing for an infidel,
Seeing featured like the Christ, believed a saint,
Sat by my pillow, charmed the sting from pain,
Quenched the fierce fever's heat, defeated Death;
And when I was made whole, had disappeared,
No man knew whither, leaving no more trace
Than a re-risen angel. This is he!'
Then Raschi, who had stood erect, nor quailed
From glances of hot hate or crazy wrath,
Now sank his eagle gaze, stooped his high head,
Veiling his glowing brow, returned the kiss
Of brother-love upon the Christian's hand,
And dropping on his knees implored the three,
'Grace for my tribe! They are what ye have made.
If any be among them fawning, false,
Insatiable, revengeful, ignorant, mean
And there are many such ask your own hearts
What virtues ye would yield for planted hate,
Ribald contempt, forced, menial servitude,
Slow centuries of vengeance for a crime
Ye never did commit? Mercy for these!
Who bear on back and breast the scathing brand
Of scarlet degradation, who are clothed
In ignominious livery, whose bowed necks
Are broken with the yoke. Change these to men!
That were a noble witchcraft simply wrought,
God's alchemy transforming clods to gold.
If there be one among them strong and wise,
Whose lips anoint breathe poetry and love,
Whose brain and heart served ever Christian need
And there are many such for his dear sake,
Lest ye chance murder one of God's high priests,
Spare his thrice-wretched tribe! Believe me, sirs,
Who have seen various lands, searched various hearts,
I have yet to touch that undiscovered shore,

Have yet to fathom that impossible soul,
Where a true benefit's forgot; where one
Slight deed of common kindness sown yields not
As now, as here, abundant crop of love.
Every good act of man, our Talmud says,
Creates an angel, hovering by his side.
Oh! what a shining host, great Duke, shall guard
Thy consecrated throne, for all the lives
Thy mercy spares, for all the tears thy ruth
Stops at the source. Behold this poor old man,
Last of a line of princes, stricken in years,
As thy dead father would have been to-day.
Was that white beard a rag for obscene hands
To tear? a weed for lumpish clowns to pluck?
Was that benignant, venerable face
Fit target for their foul throats' voided rheum?
That wrinkled flesh made to be pulled and pricked,
Wounded by flinty pebbles and keen steel?
Behold the prostrate, patriarchal form,
Bruised, silent, chained. Duke, such is Israel!'
'Unbind these men!' commanded Vladislaw.
'Go forth and still the tumult of my town.
Let no Jew suffer violence. Raschi, rise!
Thou who hast served the Christ with this priest's life,
Who is my spirit's counsellor Christ serves thee.
Return among thy people with my seal,
The talisman of safety. Let them know
The Duke's their friend. Go, publish the glad news!'
Raschi the Saviour, Raschi the Messiah,
Back to the Jewry carried peace and love.
But Narzerad fed his venomed heart with gall,
Vowing to give his fatal hatred vent,
Despite a world of weak fantastic Dukes
And heretic bishops. He fulfilled his vow.

The Death Of Raschi

[Aaron Ben Mier 'loquitur.']

If I remember Raschi? An I live,
Grandson, to bless thy grandchild, I'll forget
Never that youth and what he did for Prague.
Aye, aye, I know! he slurred a certain verse
In such and such a prayer; omitted quite
To stand erect there where the ritual
Commands us rise and bow towards the East;
Therefore, the ingrates brand him heterodox,
Neglect his memory whose virtue saved
Each knave of us alive. Not I forget,

No more does God, who wrought a miracle
For his dear sake. The Passover was here.
Raschi, just wedded with the fair Rebekah,
Bode but the lapsing of the holy week
For homeward journey with his bride to France.
The sacred meal was spread. All sat at board
Within the house of Rabbi Jochanan:
The kind old priest; his noble, new-found son,
Whose name was wrung in every key of praise,
By every voice in Prague, from Duke to serf
(Save the vindictive bigot, Narzerad);
The beautiful young wife, whose cup of joy
Sparkled at brim; next her the vacant chair
Awaited the Messiah, who, unannounced,
In God's good time shall take his place with us.
Now when the Rabbi reached the verse where one
Shall rise from table, flinging wide the door,
To give the Prophet entrance, if so be
The glorious hour have sounded, Raschi rose,
Pale, grave, yet glad with great expectancy,
Crossed the hushed room, and, with a joyous smile
To greet the Saviour, opened the door.
A curse!
A cry, 'Revenged!' a thrust, a stifled moan,
The sheathing of a poniard that was all!
In the dark vestibule a fleeing form,
Masked, gowned in black; and in the room of prayer,
Raschi, face downward on the stone-cold floor,
Bleeding his life out. Oh! what a cry was that
(Folk shuddered, hearing, roods off in the street)
Wherewith Rebekah rushed to raise her lord,
Kneeling beside him, striving in vain to quench
With turban, veil, torn shreds of gown, stained hands,
The black blood's sickening gush. He never spoke,
Never rewarded with one glance of life
The passion in her eyes. He met his end
Even as beneath the sickle the full ear
Bows to its death so beautiful, silent, ripe.

Well, we poor Jews must gulp our injuries,
Howe'er they choke us. What redress in Prague
For the inhuman murder? A strange Jew
The victim; the suspected criminal
The ducal counselor! Such odds forbade
Revenge or justice. We forbore to seek.
The priest, discrowned o' the glory of his age,
The widow-bride, mourned as though smitten of God,
Gave forth they would with solemn obsequies
Bury their dead, and crave no help from man.
Now of what chanced betwixt the night of murder
And the appointed burial I can give

Only the sum of gossip servants' tales,
Neighbors' reports, close confidences leaked
From friends and kindred. Night and day, folk said,
Rebekah wept, prayed, fasted by the corpse,
Three mortal days. Upon the third, her eyes,
Sunk in their pits, glimmered with wild, strange fire.
She started from her place beside the dead,
Kissed clay-cold brow, cheeks, lids, and lips once more,
And with a maniac's wan, heart-breaking smile,
Veiled, hooded, glided through the twilight streets,
A sable shadow. From the willow-grove,
Close by the Moldau's brink, beyond the bridge,
Her trace was lost. 'T was evening and mild May,
Air full of spring, skies perfect as a pearl;
Yet one who saw her pass amidst the shades
O' the blue-gray branches swears a sudden flame,
As of miraculous lightning, thrilled through heaven.
One hour thereafter she reentered Prague,
Slid swiftly through the streets, as though borne on
By ankle-wings or floating on soft cloud,
Smiling no more, but with illumined eyes,
Transfigured brow, grave lips, and faltering limbs,
So came into the room where Raschi lay
Stretched 'twixt tall tapers lit at head and foot.
She held in both hands leafy, flowerless plants,
Some she had fastened in her twisted hair,
Stuck others in her girdle, and from all
Issued a racy odor, pungent-sweet,
The living soul of Spring. Death's chamber seemed
As though clear sunshine and a singing bird
Therein had entered. From the precious herb
She poured into a golden bowl the sap,
Sparkling like wine; then with a soundless prayer,
White as the dead herself, she held the cup
To Raschi's mouth. A quick, small flame sprang up
From the enchanted balsam, died away,
And lo! the color dawned in cheek and lips,
The life returned, the sealed, blind lids were raised,
And in the glorious eyes love reawoke,
And, looking up, met love.
                            So runs the tale,
Mocked by the worldly-wise; but I believe,
Knowing the miracles the Lord hath wrought
In every age for Jacob's seed. Moreover,
I, with the highest and meanest Jew in Prague,
Was at the burial. No man saw the dead.
Sealed was the coffin ere the rites began,
And none could swear it went not empty down
Into the hollow earth. Too shrewd our priest
To publish such a wonder, and expose
That consecrated life to second death.

Scarce were the thirty days of mourning sped,
When we awoke to find his home left bare,
Rebekah and her father fled from Prague.
God grant they had glad meeting otherwhere!

Saint Romualdo

I give God thanks that I, a lean old man,
Wrinkled, infirm, and crippled with keen pains
By austere penance and continuous toil,
Now rest in spirit, and possess 'the peace
Which passeth understanding.' Th' end draws nigh,
Though the beginning is yesterday,
And a broad lifetime spreads 'twixt this and that
A favored life, though outwardly the butt
Of ignominy, malice, and affront,
Yet lighted from within by the clear star
Of a high aim, and graciously prolonged
To see at last its utmost goal attained.
I speak not of mine Order and my House,
Here founded by my hands and filled with saints
A white society of snowy souls,
Swayed by my voice, by mine example led;
For this is but the natural harvest reaped
From labors such as mine when blessed by God.
Though I rejoice to think my spirit still
Will work my purposes, through worthy hands,
After my bones are shriveled into dust,
Yet have I gleaned a finer, sweeter fruit
Of holy satisfaction, sure and real,
Though subtler than the tissue of the air
The power completely to detach the soul
From her companion through this life, the flesh;
So that in blessed privacy of peace,
Communing with high angels, she can hold,
Serenely rapt, her solitary course.

Ye know, O saints of heaven, what I have borne
Of discipline and scourge; the twisted lash
Of knotted rope that striped my shrinking limbs;
Vigils and fasts protracted, till my flesh
Wasted and crumbled from mine aching bones,
And the last skin, one woof of pain and sores,
Thereto like yellow parchment loosely clung;
Exposure to the fever and the frost,
When 'mongst the hollows of the hills I lurked
From persecution of misguided folk,
Accustoming my spirit to ignore
The burden of the cross, while picturing

The bliss of disembodied souls, the grace
Of holiness, the lives of sainted men,
And entertaining all exalted thoughts,
That nowise touched the trouble of the hour,
Until the grief and pain seemed far less real
Than the creations of my brain inspired.
The vision, the beatitude, were true:
The agony was but an evil dream.
I speak not now as one who hath not learned
The purport of those lightly-bandied words,
Evil and Fate, but rather one who knows
The thunders of the terrors of the world.
No mortal chance or change, no earthly shock,
Can move or reach my soul, securely throned
On heights of contemplation and calm prayer,
Happy, serene, no less actual joy
Of present peace than faith in joys to come.

This soft, sweet, yellow evening, how the trees
Stand crisp against the clear, bright-colored sky!
How the white mountain-tops distinctly shine,
Taking and giving radiance, and the slopes
Are purpled with rich floods of peach-hued light!
Thank God, my filmy, old dislustred eyes
Find the same sense of exquisite delight,
My heart vibrates to the same touch of joy
In scenes like this, as when my pulse danced high,
And youth coursed through my veins! This the one link
That binds the wan old man that now I am
To the wild lad who followed up the hounds
Among Ravenna's pine-woods by the sea.
For there how oft would I lose all delight
In the pursuit, the triumph, or the game,
To stray alone among the shadowy glades,
And gaze, as one who is not satisfied
With gazing, at the large, bright, breathing sea,
The forest glooms, and shifting gleams between
The fine dark fringes of the fadeless trees,
On gold-green turf, sweet-brier, and wild pink rose!
How rich that buoyant air with changing scent
Of pungent pine, fresh flowers, and salt cool seas!
And when all echoes of the chase had died,
Of horn and halloo, bells and baying hounds,
How mine ears drank the ripple of the tide
On the fair shore, the chirp of unseen birds,
The rustling of the tangled undergrowth,
And the deep lyric murmur of the pines,
When through their high tops swept the sudden breeze!
There was my world, there would my heart dilate,
And my aspiring soul dissolve in prayer
Unto that Spirit of Love whose energies

Were active round me, yet whose presence, sphered
In the unsearchable, unbodied air,
Made itself felt, but reigned invisible.
This ere the day that made me what I am.
Still can I see the hot, bright sky, the sea
Illimitably sparkling, as they showed
That morning. Though I deemed I took no note
Of heaven or earth or waters, yet my mind
Retains to-day the vivid portraiture
Of every line and feature of the scene.
Light-hearted 'midst the dewy lanes I fared
Unto the sea, whose jocund gleam I caught
Between the slim boles, when I heard the clink
Of naked weapons, then a sudden thrust
Sickening to hear, and then a stifled groan;
And pressing forward I beheld the sight
That seared itself for ever on my brain
My kinsman, Ser Ranieri, on the turf,
Fallen upon his side, his bright young head
Among the pine-spurs, and his cheek pressed close
Unto the moist, chill sod: his fingers clutched
A handful of loose weeds and grass and earth,
Uprooted in his anguish as he fell,
And slowly from his heart the thick stream flowed,
Fouling the green, leaving the fair, sweet face
Ghastly, transparent, with blue, stony eyes
Staring in blankness on that other one
Who triumphed over him. With hot desire
Of instant vengeance I unsheathed my sword
To rush upon the slayer, when he turned
In his first terror of blood-guiltiness.

Within my heart a something snapped and brake.
What was it but the chord of rapturous joy
For ever stilled? I tottered and would fall,
Had I not leaned against the friendly pine;
For all realities of life, unmoored
From their firm anchorage, appeared to float
Like hollow phantoms past my dizzy brain.
The strange delusion wrought upon my soul
That this had been enacted ages since.
This very horror curdled at my heart,
This net of trees spread round, these iron heavens,
Were closing over me when I had stood,
Unnumbered cycles back, and fronted HIM,
My father; and he felt mine eyes as now,
Yet saw me not; and then, as now, that form,
The one thing real, lay stretched between us both.
The fancy passed, and I stood sane and strong
To grasp the truth. Then I remembered all

A few fierce words between them yester eve
Concerning some poor plot of pasturage,
Soon silenced into courteous, frigid calm:
This was the end. I could not meet him now,
To curse him, to accuse him, or to save,
And draw him from the red entanglement
Coiled by his own hands round his ruined life.
God pardon me! My heart that moment held
No drop of pity toward this wretched soul;
And cowering down, as though his guilt were mine,
I fled amidst the savage silences
Of that grim wood, resolved to nurse alone
My boundless desolation, shame, and grief.
There, in that thick-leaved twilight of high noon,
The quiet of the still, suspended air,
Once more my wandering thoughts were calmly ranged,
Shepherded by my will. I wept, I prayed
A solemn prayer, conceived in agony,
Blessed with response instant, miraculous;
For in that hour my spirit was at one
With Him who knows and satisfies her needs.
The supplication and the blessing sprang
From the same source, inspired divinely both.
I prayed for light, self-knowledge, guidance, truth,
And these like heavenly manna were rained down
To feed my hungered soul. His guilt was mine.
What angel had been sent to stay mine arm
Until the fateful moment passed away
That would have ushered an eternity
Of withering remorse? I found the germs
In mine own heart of every human sin,
That waited but occasion's tempting breath
To overgrow with poisoned bloom my life.
What God thus far had saved me from myself?
Here was the lofty truth revealed, that each
Must feel himself in all, must know where'er
The great soul acts or suffers or enjoys,
His proper soul in kinship there is bound.
Then my life-purpose dawned upon my mind,
Encouraging as morning. As I lay,
Crushed by the weight of universal love,
Which mine own thoughts had heaped upon myself,
I heard the clear chime of a slow, sweet bell.
I knew it whence it came and what it sang.
From the gray convent nigh the wood it pealed,
And called the monks to prayer. Vigil and prayer,
Clean lives, white days of strict austerity:
Such were the offerings of these holy saints.
How far might such not tend to expiate
A riotous world's indulgence? Here my life,
Doubly austere and doubly sanctified,

Might even for that other one atone,
So bound to mine, till both should be forgiven.

They sheltered me, not questioning the need
That led me to their cloistered solitude.
How rich, how freighted with pure influence,
With dear security of perfect peace,
Was the first day I passed within those walls!
The holy habit of perpetual prayer,
The gentle greetings, the rare temperate speech,
The chastening discipline, the atmosphere
Of settled and profound tranquillity,
Were even as living waters unto one
Who perisheth of thirst. Was this the world
That yesterday seemed one huge battlefield
For brutish passions? Could the soul of man
Withdraw so easily, and erect apart
Her own fair temple for her own high ends?
But this serene contentment slowly waned
As I discerned the broad disparity
Betwixt the form and spirit of the laws
That bound the order in strait brotherhood.
Yet when I sought to gain a larger love,
More rigid discipline, severer truth,
And more complete surrender of the soul
Unto her God, this was to my reproach,
And scoffs and gibes beset me on all sides.
In mine own cell I mortified my flesh,
I held aloof from all my brethren's feasts
To wrestle with my viewless enemies,
Till they should leave their blessing on my head;
For nightly was I haunted by that face,
White, bloodless, as I saw it 'midst the ferns,
Now staring out of darkness, and it held
Mine eyes from slumber and my brain from rest
And drove me from my straw to weep and pray.
Rebellious thoughts such subtle torture wrought
Upon my spirit that I lay day-long
In dumb despair, until the blessed hope
Of mercy dawned again upon my soul,
As gradual as the slow gold moon that mounts
The airy steps of heaven. My faith arose
With sure perception that disaster, wrong,
And every shadow of man's destiny
Are merely circumstance, and cannot touch
The soul's fine essence: they exist or die
Only as she affirms them or denies.

This faith sustain me even to the end:
It floods my heart with peace as surely now
As on that day the friars drove me forth,

Urging that my asceticism, too harsh,
Endured through pride, would bring into reproach
Their customs and their order. Then began
My exile in the mountains, where I bode
A hunted man. The elements conspired
Against me, and I was the seasons' sport,
Drenched, parched, and scorched and frozen alternately,
Burned with shrewd frosts, prostrated by fierce heats,
Shivering 'neath chilling dews and gusty rains,
And buffeted by all the winds of heaven.
Yet was this period my time of joy:
My daily thoughts perpetual converse held
With angels ministrant; mine ears were charmed
With sweet accordance of celestial sounds,
Song, harp and choir, clear ringing through the air.
And visions were revealed unto mine eyes
By night and day of Heaven's very courts,
In shadowless, undimmed magnificence.
I gave God thanks, not that He sheltered me,
And fed me as He feeds the fowls of air
For had I perished, this too had been well
But for the revelation of His truth,
The glory, the beatitude vouchsafed
To exalt, to heal, to quicken, to inspire;
So that the pinched, lean excommunicate
Was crowned with joy more solid, more secure,
Than all the comfort of the vales could bring.
Then the good Lord touched certain fervid hearts,
Aspiring toward His love, to come to me,
Timid and few at first; but as they heard
From mine own lips the precious oracles,
That soothed the trouble of their souls, appeased
Their spiritual hunger, and disclosed
All of the God within them to themselves,
They flocked about me, and they hailed me saint,
And sware to follow and to serve the good
Which my word published and my life declared.
Thus the lone hermit of the mountain-top
Descended leader of a band of saints,
And midway 'twixt the summit and the vale
I perched my convent. Yet I bated not
One whit of strict restraint and abstinence.
And they who love me and who serve the truth
Have learned to suffer with me, and have won
The supreme joy that is not of the flesh,
Foretasting the delights of Paradise.
This faith, to them imparted, will endure
After my tongue hath ceased to utter it,
And the great peace hath settled on my soul.